Ste. Genevieve, Missouri

A Walk through History

By Valerie Battle Kienzle

Foreword by Bill Hart

REEDY PRESS

Copyright © 2024 Reedy Press, LLC

Reedy Press
PO Box 5131
St. Louis, MO 63139
reedypress.com

Front cover images:
Main image: courtesy of Eridony (Instagram: eridony_prime).
Bottom images, from left to right: Library of Congress, public domain;
Library of Congress, public domain; Valerie Battle Kienzle; Valerie Battle Kienzle;
Library of Congress, public domain; Valerie Battle Kienzle.

Cover and interior design: Eric Marquard

ISBN: 9781681065090

Printed in the United States
24 25 26 27 28 5 4 3 2 1

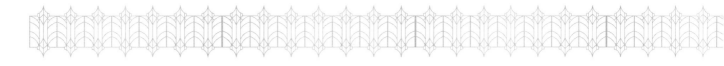

Hubardeau Icehouse
COURTESY OF
VALERIE BATTLE KIENZLE

Old Post Office
COURTESY OF LIBRARY
OF CONGRESS, PUBLIC DOMAIN

A crowd gathers to watch
the first railroad train arrive
in Ste. Genevieve, 1899
COURTESY OF MISSOURI
HISTORICAL SOCIETY, ST. LOUIS

Contents

Foreword

History is indeed a journey through place and time. When even a familiar place's story is told and its history further discovered, though we may have experienced it a hundred times, it can seem that we are discovering it for the very first time. We are immensely enriched by how we are guided through this history. Valerie Battle Kienzle is no stranger to walking us through history—both temporal and physical. Her work here is quite literally a walk through the city and history of Ste. Genevieve, Missouri.

Most of us learn about the early history of the United States when we are children. We learn about the "13 original colonies" and therefore we tend to think that the area of Colonial America is confined to the Eastern Seaboard. Founded only three years after Georgia, the final one of these original colonies, was the settlement of Ste. Genevieve. What is now Middle America seems an unlikely canvas on which to paint an architectural history of Colonial America, but it exists right here and is pictured very well in this volume.

The architectural legacy of Ste. Genevieve is remarkable in that it offers some of the rarest examples of French Colonial vernacular architecture in North America. The significance of these buildings cannot be overstated. These guided tours of Ste. Genevieve offer an interesting and informative look at the history west of the Mississippi through its remarkably preserved built environment, and their format makes the journey a part of the experience. Carefully researched studies of buildings, their architecture, and the people who built them greet the reader as we take this amazing walk through time.

—BILL HART

Bill Hart is director emeritus of the Missouri Alliance for Historic Preservation and currently director of the Perry County, Missouri, Historical Society. Long active in preservation of the built environment and French culture in Missouri, he has been involved on the boards of the Chatillon-DeMenil House Foundation and Les Amis French cultural organization, which promotes the French Cultural Corridor on both sides of the Mississippi River from St. Louis to Ste. Genevieve. Having grown up in small-town Missouri, he has a particular interest in its history and authored the book Historic Missouri Roadsides. *In its second edition from Reedy Press, the book is a road-trip guide to small-town Missouri on two-lane highways, promoting heritage tourism in the state's small towns and villages.*

Downtown mural on 380 Market Street designed and painted by Joy French
COURTESY OF VALERIE BATTLE KIENZLE

Introduction

Ste. Genevieve contains one of the oldest and finest examples of an authentic French Colonial village in the United States. It was the first permanent settlement in Missouri and was named for Sainte Geneviève, the fifth-century patron saint of Paris, France.

Its more recent development began in 17th-century Canada. Québec authorities chose René-Robert Cavelier de La Salle to lead an exploratory expedition down the Mississippi River. The ultimate goal was to claim the Mississippi Valley lands for France's King Louis XIV. It operated under first the French flag and then the Spanish flag before returning to French control in 1800. In 1803, the area became part of the Louisiana Purchase, the massive land transfer from France that doubled the size of the US.

Following the river, French Canadians traveled south and settled in Cahokia (c. 1699) and Kaskaskia (c. 1703) in today's Illinois. The original Ste. Genevieve has become referred to as *Le Vieux Village* (The Old Town). Opportunities for agricultural expansion led some to look to the agricultural benefits of the fertile river bottomland (alluvial plains) across the river. Flooding was an ongoing problem at The Old Town site due to its location on the riverbank. Crops were destroyed in a major 1785 flood (*l'année des grandes eaux*—the year of the great flood) and areas filled with silt. This led to gradual relocation and resettlement several miles inland from the river, between the north and south branches of Gabouri Creek (*La Petite Rivière Gabouri*). The new town was called *Nouvelle Ste. Genevieve* (New Ste. Genevieve).

Ste. Genevieve's first land grants were awarded in the 1740s. Another grant was awarded in 1751. A large common field area of approximately 7,000 acres called *Le Grand Champ* (The Big Field) was divided into long, narrow lots measured in arpents. (A square arpent is approximately .85 acre.) Individual lots measured one to three arpents wide by 40 arpents long, or approximately 34 to 102 acres per lot. Some lots were larger; others were smaller. Settlers established orchards and grew all types of fruits and vegetables. The village's population grew following the Seven Years' War (1754–1763), also known as the French and Indian War. By 1773, the population was about 670.

Ste. Genevieve's late-18th-century growth paralleled that of St. Louis, approximately 60 miles north, but St. Louis's population began to outpace Ste. Genevieve's following the Louisiana Purchase. St. Louis became the center of Midwest commercial trade.

Missouri became the Territory of Louisiana in 1804 with a governor and the Territory of Missouri in 1812. It became a state in 1821. Ste. Genevieve became one of Missouri's five original territorial districts. By the 1840s, the French-dominated city welcomed immigrants of other ethnicities, including individuals from the Black Forest region of southwestern Germany and Anglo-Americans.

Salt springs and lead mines had been discovered nearby long before Ste. Genevieve was founded. Both had been used by Native Americans and early French settlers on the east side of the Mississippi River. These important commodities would later be mined by the Ste. Genevieve Lime and Quarry Company, the Western Lime Works, and the Peerless White Lime Company in the early 20th century and shipped to various locales via the Mississippi River and railroads.

Today's population is approximately 5,000. Thanks to a group of forward-thinking mid-20th-century residents, Ste. Genevieve's rich French Colonial heritage and many of its centuries-old buildings have been preserved. In 2020, three significant properties in the historic area became Ste. Genevieve National Historical Park, the 422nd unit of the National Park Service. Parts of the city were named a National Historic Landmark District in 1960 and numerous properties are included in the National Register of Historic Places. Annual festivals and traditional celebrations invite visitors to step back in time and learn about the area's early heritage. And what better way to experience historic Ste. Genevieve's sights and sounds than on foot?

You may notice variations in the spellings and use of accents in names throughout this book, including that of Ste. Genevieve itself, which has added and removed its accent since its founding. In an effort to be as historically accurate as possible, we have made these adjustments based on the time period referenced in the text.

From the Beginning . . .

Entrance to Ste. Genevieve National Park Service Headquarters, St. Marys Road.
COURTESY OF VALERIE BATTLE KIENZLE

Information Gathering

❖ To get a broad understanding of the history of Ste. Genevieve, stop by the **Ste. Genevieve/Great River Road Welcome Center, 66 South Main and Market Streets**. The parking lot entrance is behind the Welcome Center off of Market Street, or you can park along Market or Main Streets.

The Welcome Center is open every day from 9 a.m. until 5 p.m. It offers maps, information on area attractions and special events, tours, lodging information, and local history displays. Whether this is your first or 20th visit, the Welcome Center is the perfect place to find the latest information about all things Ste. Genevieve. The building also features an extensive diorama display depicting Ste. Genevieve c. 1832. The detailed diorama measures 9' by 11' and was meticulously handcrafted at 1:225 scale by late local scale modeler Lewis Pruneau. It features more than 100 house and building re-creations. It was commissioned by Les Amis-Saint Louis, a nonprofit 501(c)(3) organization that promotes the preservation of the French Creole heritage and culture in the mid–Mississippi River Valley.

Introductory Driving Tour

After gathering materials, return to your vehicle. Exercise caution as some area streets have no sidewalks or crosswalks. The first part of this tour is best completed in your vehicle as considerable distances exist between the various historical sites. Throughout this part of the tour and the walking tours, please be respectful of others. Some of the historic buildings and homes are private residences and are located on private property. Others are part of Ste. Genevieve National Historical Park, the 422nd unit of the National Park Service, and are open only during certain hours. All National Park Service homes are fee-free. Other properties run by partner organizations may charge entrance fees. Check signs at each location or online for specific information.

Once in your vehicle, head south on Main Street. Travel under the railroad bridge and continue south as it becomes St. Marys Road. Stay on St. Marys for approximately 0.7 mile until arriving at the **Jean Baptiste Vallé/Pierre Dorlac House, 389 St. Marys Rd.** (*Note: A small stone fence sits near the roadway and in front of the house.*)

Jean Baptiste Vallé/ Pierre Dorlac House

389 St. Marys Rd. (Private residence)

PREFACE *The Vallé name has been associated with Ste. Genevieve since its early founding. The Vallés originated in Beauport, a village in the vicinity of Québec. François Vallé moved to Kaskaskia, Illinois, in the 1740s and eventually relocated across the Mississippi River to Ste. Genevieve. He and his wife had five children. They prospered and became the area's wealthiest residents. Ste. Genevieve came under Spanish rule in 1762, and, unlike many local residents, Vallé befriended Spanish authority Don Pedro Piernas and his troops. Vallé subsequently*

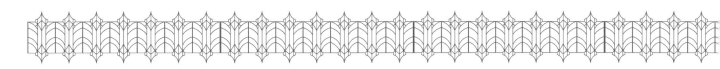

COURTESY OF
VALERIE BATTLE KIENZLE

was appointed Captain of the Militia of Ste. Genevieve. He served until his death in 1783. He was succeeded by several individuals until his son François Vallé II was named civil and military commandant in 1796. By that time, area residents had tired of routine flooding and relocated the settlement to drier land several miles inland from the river. The Vallé name is found on several houses on this tour.

Pierre Dorlac owned this property in 1790. He was the son of some of Ste. Genevieve's earliest settlers, François Dorlac and Françoise Phillipaux. He died in 1803. His widow and her second husband sold the property in 1806 to Jean Baptiste Vallé and his wife, Catherine Moreau. They built this house c. 1807. He was the nephew of the local commandant with the same name and a grandson of François Vallé. This transitional house has French Creole–style vertical log construction (*poteaux-sur-sol*) on a limestone foundation with *bouzillage* (mixture of clay, grass, and rocks used as fill or chinking), but also shows some Anglo-American touches. It was remodeled with Greek Revival characteristics. The house faces east toward the original agricultural plots and flood plain near the Mississippi River.

 After viewing the house's exterior, turn your vehicle around and go back up St. Marys Road.

Le Grand Champ
St. Marys Road

❖ *Le Grand Champ* contained thousands of acres of fertile agriculture fields that stretched along the Mississippi River. *Le Grand Champ* represents a communal type of farming favored by the early

residents of Ste. Genevieve in which fences did not separate privately owned farm plots. The rich acreage has been used for centuries for agricultural cultivation. One part of it contains a Native American mound standing 16 feet tall. Archaeological investigations were conducted around the mound in 2009 by a graduate student from Indiana. The mound has been dated back to the Mississippian Period and likely is connected to the mounds in nearby Cahokia, Illinois. No excavations have been conducted on the mound.

Jean Baptiste Bequette-Ribault House
351 St. Marys Rd. (Open to the public by appointment)

❖ This *poteaux-en-terre* house (vertical logs in the ground) with typical French Norman support trusses was built by Jean Baptiste Bequette Sr. and dates back

COURTESY OF
LIBRARY OF CONGRESS, PUBLIC DOMAIN

to 1808. It is one of three original *poteaux-en-terre* structures in Ste. Genevieve. Only five such structures remain in the US. Its restoration provided architectural historians with an in-depth look at 18th-century French Creole construction techniques. It has a raised *galerie* (porch) on all sides. Clarisse Ribault, a free woman of color, purchased the home in 1840. It remained in the Ribault family for several generations. It is listed in the National Register of Historic Places and is open for tours by reservation.

Lasource-Durand House
347 St. Marys Rd.
(Behind the Bequette-Ribault House, open to the public by appointment)

❖ This tiny, unrestored c. 1814 French Creole–style cabin was moved here in the mid-1980s from its

COURTESY OF LIBRARY OF CONGRESS, PUBLIC DOMAIN

original location to avoid demolition. It is an example of French Colonial *poteaux-sur-sol* and *pierrotage* (stones and/or clay and mortar used as filler between wooden framing posts) construction. It has a limestone foundation and had a fireplace that included a bake oven. The original structure was a one-room cabin with two windows, doors, and porches on the front and back. An early addition was dismantled and stored.

 After viewing the houses' exteriors, resume travel on St. Marys Road.

Bauvais-Amoureux House

327 St. Marys Rd.

❖ The Bauvais-Amoureux House is owned and operated by Ste. Genevieve National Historical Park. This French Creole–style house was built c. 1792 by Jean Baptiste St. Gemme Bauvais II, who had relocated across the Mississippi River from Kaskaskia. He was a brother of Vital St. Gemme Bauvais. The house is one of Ste. Genevieve's three surviving *poteaux-en-terre* buildings and one of five surviving French Canadian vernacular structures in the US. Outside stairs provide access to the upper level. Pélagie and Benjamin Amoureux obtained the house in 1852 and raised their family there. Visit the National Park Service Welcome Center to arrange tours.

 After viewing the house's exterior, resume travel on St. Marys Road.

William Brooks House/Sassafras Creek Originals & Telle-Frentzel House

311 St. Marys Rd. (Private residence)

❖ This c. 1850 building is one of two remaining residences from Ste. Genevieve's early African American community. A free man named Casimere lived in this two-story, wood-framed vernacular house on a raised limestone foundation. The house was occupied by William Brooks until his death in 1983. Today it

houses Sassafras Creek Originals, an Early American furniture and decor store. The store's owner relocated the Telle-Frentzel House/Granary, a c. 1840 cabin, from Perry County to the William Brooks House property. The cabin was carefully dismantled and reconstructed. Neither structure has the traditional French vertical log construction found in many of Ste. Genevieve's Colonial-Era buildings.

 Resume travel on St. Marys Road to the four-way-stop intersection at Seraphin Street.

COURTESY OF VALERIE BATTLE KIENZLE

BONUS SIDE TRIP

At the four-way-stop intersection, turn left onto Seraphin Street. Drive a short distance to 74 Seraphin Street on the left.

Joseph Seraphin House

74 Seraphin St. (Private residence)

❖ Some of the original details of this c. 1826 French vertical log house have been covered by modern materials. The original house was built on stone piers, with the space between the piers filled in with more stone, *poteaux-sur-sol*. The original foundation is stone. Researchers say this is the only 1½-story Creole house in the area that was originally built with an upper story. Joseph Seraphin owned the property and sold it in 1826 to a free African American, Antoine Racola. The property was sold at auction to John L. Bogy in 1873.

To resume the Driving Tour, travel back along Seraphin Street to the four-way-stop intersection and turn left onto St. Marys Road.

COURTESY OF
VALERIE BATTLE KIENZLE

Green Tree Tavern/
Nicolas Janis-Ziegler House
244 St. Marys Rd. (Visit the National Park
Service Welcome Center for tours)

❖ The Green Tree Tavern/Nicolas Janis-Ziegler House, part of the Ste. Genevieve National Historical Park, is said to be the city's oldest house. Nicolas and Marie Janis relocated to Ste. Genevieve from Kaskaskia about 1789. They built this French Colonial *poteaux-sur-sol* with *bouzillage* house about 1790–91. Dendrochronology (a technique for dating the felling date of wood construction material using the spacing of the tree rings) was used on pieces of the house to arrive at that date. The house varies from similar houses because it includes unique triple fireplaces

COURTESY OF
LIBRARY OF CONGRESS,
PUBLIC DOMAIN

with one common flue. It features a wraparound *galerie* and raised basement. The structure was deeded to François Janis by Nicholas in 1796. He operated it as an inn and tavern. It was sold in 1833 to German immigrant Mathias Ziegler. The family lived there into the 20th century.

Dr. Aaron Elliott House
207 South Main St. (La Grande Rue, private
residence)

❖ The construction date for the original part of this house is c. 1806. This part still contains many of its original building components. Additions were made to the house later in the 19th century, including a second story. It has a limestone rubble foundation and is covered with wood shingles. It is part of the Ste.

Genevieve Historic District and is listed in the National Register of Historic Places. Aaron Elliott was married to Gloriana Austin Elliott, sister of another Ste. Genevieve resident, Moses Austin, whose son Stephen founded Austin, Texas.

✦ Note that St. Marys Road comes to a fork near the crossing over South Gabouri Creek and under the railroad tracks. To continue this tour, follow the road to the right as it crosses the creek and continues as South Main Street.

Railroad Bridge over South Main Street
❖ This steel girder Missouri–Illinois Railroad Bridge crosses over South Main Street at a distinct angle and joins spans that carry the railroad tracks across the South Fork of the Gabouri Creek. The bridge's west abutment shows a 1901 construction date. The first train arrived in Ste. Genevieve in June 1899. Trains became an important mode of transportation in Ste. Genevieve.

✦ This concludes the Introductory Driving Tour. To begin Tour 1, return to the Ste. Genevieve/ Great River Road Welcome Center at 66 South Main and Market Streets. Park in the lot behind the Center off Market Street or along Market or Main Streets.

COURTESY OF
VALERIE BATTLE KIENZLE

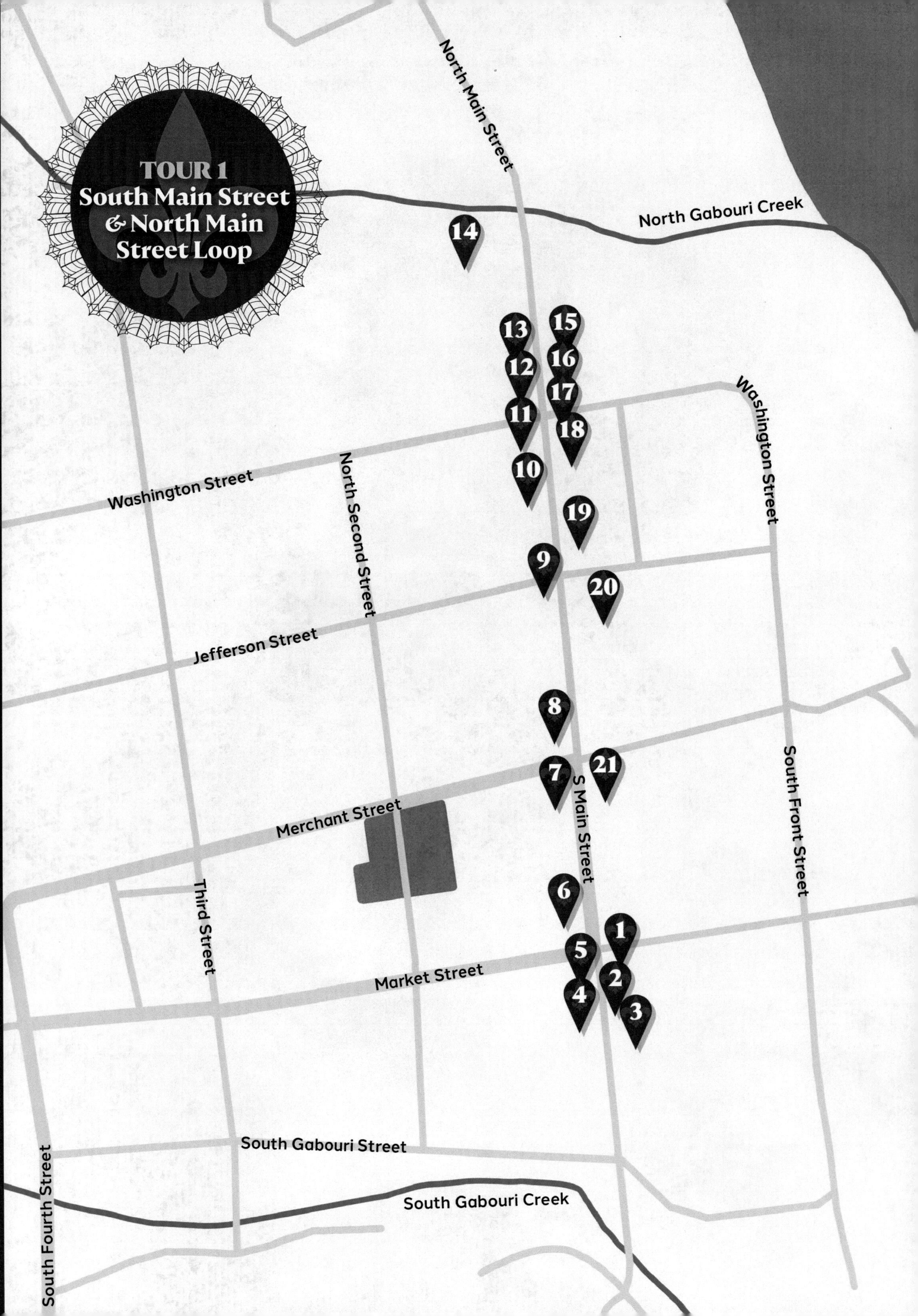
TOUR 1
South Main Street & North Main Street Loop
North Main Street
North Gabouri Creek
Washington Street
Washington Street
North Second Street
Jefferson Street
Merchant Street
S Main Street
South Front Street
Third Street
Market Street
South Gabouri Street
South Gabouri Creek
South Fourth Street
1
2
3
4
5
6
7
8
9
10
11
12
13
14
15
16
17
18
19
20
21

TOUR 1
South Main Street
& North Main Street Loop
Approximately 1 mile

✴ This walking tour begins on South Main Street *(La Grande Rue)* at the parking lot for the Ste. Genevieve/Great River Road Welcome Center at 66 South Main and Market Streets. The parking lot entrance is behind the Welcome Center off Market Street, or you can park along Market or Main Street. If you have not done so already, step inside the Welcome Center for brochures, maps, and helpful people who can answer questions. To begin Tour 1, exit the Welcome Center and turn right onto Market Street. Follow Market a short distance to its intersection with South Main Street. Turn left down South Main to the brick house on the corner.

① Joseph Nicholas Amoureux/ Etienne Parent House

102 South Main St. (Private residence)

❖ This c. 1844 brick house is an example of Anglo-American architecture. It has a limestone foundation, like many Ste. Genevieve houses, and features a

stepped parapet front. It also has exterior Greek Revival elements and some original woodwork. During restoration work, it was discovered that the house's original front door and a window had been switched and reconfigured.

COURTESY OF VALERIE BATTLE KIENZLE

② Hands-On History at the Linden House/Gemien Bauvais House

116 South Main St.

❖ The Centre for French Colonial Life operates Hands-On History at the Linden House/Gemien Bauvais House as one of its three historic house museums. Its featured hands-on history activities allow children and adults to experience French Colonial life through a

COURTESY OF VALERIE BATTLE KIENZLE

variety of educational activities and crafts. These include a schoolroom, a vintage store, and the use of a bow and arrow. Gemien (Jemmien) Bauvais bought this lot in 1811. The Gemien Bauvais/Linden House was built c. 1813 and has been enlarged and modified through the years. It gets its current name from a huge linden tree once located on the property. The property also includes 200-plus-year-old boxwood bushes.

③ Antoine O'Neille House/ The Silversmith's House

150 South Main St. (Privately owned by the Presbyterian Church)

❖ Antoine O'Neille purchased this lot in 1810. A house is thought to have been built here c. 1818–1820.

COURTESY OF VALERIE BATTLE KIENZLE

A Walk through History · 1

O'Neille had worked as a silversmith in Vincennes, Indiana, prior to relocating to Ste. Genevieve. This house, like many Ste. Genevieve houses, most likely had additions and modifications made to it through the years by various owners. The original structure of this Anglo-American vernacular timber I-house was thought to be a single story. At some point, a half story was added. A fire damaged the house in 1982, and it remained unoccupied for many years. It has since been restored. The house is listed in the National Register of Historic Places.

 Cross South Main Street to the next sites.

COURTESY OF
LIBRARY OF CONGRESS, PUBLIC DOMAIN

4 Louis Bolduc House
135 South Main St.

❖ This French Colonial *poteaux-sur-sol* construction dates to the late 18th century. Louis Bolduc, miner, merchant, and planter, relocated from the original Ste. Genevieve near the river to the new town in the 1790s. Some wood may have been salvaged from a structure located at the original site. *Maison Bolduc* features the wraparound *galerie* favored by the French and has a stockade fence. Whitewashed walls reflected heat. The Bolduc family lived here into the 20th century. This was Ste. Genevieve's first meticulously restored historic structure. It is furnished with period pieces and is operated as part of the Centre for French Colonial Life. It was added to the National Register of Historic Places in 1969 and was designated a National Historic Landmark in 1970.

COURTESY OF
VALERIE BATTLE KIENZLE

5 Bolduc–LeMeilleur House
125 South Main St.

❖ René LeMeilleur was married to Louis Bolduc's granddaughter. This one-story timber-framed house, built c. 1820, is an example of transitional architectural styles from French Colonial vertical log construction to Anglo-American. It has two front and rear doors, front and rear galleries, and a limestone rubble foundation. LeMeilleur died soon after completion of the house. It then passed to Catherine Bolduc, his mother-in-law and the widow of Etienne Bolduc. It was acquired by Jean Baptiste Vallé, who in 1837 gave it to the Sisters of Loretto. They used it for many years. A second story had been added but was removed during the house's renovation. This building is another of the historic house museums operated by the Centre for French Colonial Life.

6 Jean Baptiste Vallé House
99 South Main St. at Market St.

❖ Jean Baptiste Vallé's house was built c. 1794 with French-style *poteaux-sur-sol* construction, a large wraparound *galerie*, and a rose garden and arbor.

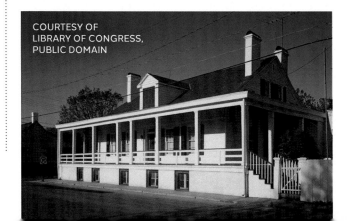

COURTESY OF
LIBRARY OF CONGRESS,
PUBLIC DOMAIN

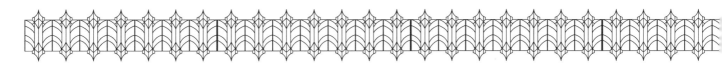

Vallé was one of four sons of François Vallé I and Marianne Billeron. He served as interim commandant and captain of the militia from February 6 until March 10, 1804, when he was named commandant. He held that position for six months until October 1, 1804. His house was both home and a government center. The Vallé family prospered in mining and mercantile ventures. A private residence until 2010, it has undergone renovations throughout its existence. It is a tour home. See the NPS Welcome Center for tours.

⑦ Pocket Park/Former Site of Merchant's Bank of Ste. Genevieve/ Ste. Genevieve Savings Bank
1 South Main St. at Merchant St.

❖ John Firman Rozier and his cashier opened the Merchant's Bank of Ste. Genevieve on Tuesday morning, May 27, 1873. Two gun-wielding members of a gang followed them into the bank. Three others remained on guard outside. The bank's safe was opened and the thieves took about $4,000, a large amount at that time.

COURTESY OF VALERIE BATTLE KIENZLE

The robbers were never caught. The building has since been razed and replaced by a small arbor and shelter. A commemorative marker was placed on a nearby shelter in 2010 by the Sons of Union Veterans of the Civil War and the St. Louis Civil War Round Table.

⑧ Audubon's Hotel/Hotel Ste. Genevieve
**9 North Main St. at Merchant St.
(Privately owned B&B)**

❖ If the walls of the Audubon's Hotel, Audubon's Palace Bar, and Audubon's Restaurant could talk, what a colorful story they could tell of 20th-century life in this

COURTESY OF VALERIE BATTLE KIENZLE

river city. Audubon's story begins in 1903, when work was completed on a large brick building at the corner of Main and Merchant Streets. The Palace Bar opened. The City Hotel and Gem Lunch Room opened the following year. Unfortunately, poor financial choices led to the building's closure in 1906, but City Hotel reopened under new management in 1907. Soon a barbershop and plumbing company also were located in the sizable building. The building has witnessed its share of events, including various owners, name changes, fire, and Ste. Genevieve's first television. Today, the Audubon complex offers a welcoming ambiance for visitors.

⑨ Dr. Hertich House
99 North Main St. (Privately owned B&B)

❖ Dr. Charles S. Hertich was born in Ste. Genevieve in 1821 to Joseph Hertich. He studied medicine in Burlington, Iowa, and at the St. Louis Medical College before serving as a surgeon to Native Americans in Minnesota. He returned to Ste. Genevieve, married

COURTESY OF VALERIE BATTLE KIENZLE

Mary Rozier, and practiced medicine until 1878. His house was built c. 1850 and was later remodeled with Second Empire Victorian ornamentation. The house featured two cupboards built into the wall between the two ground-floor rooms. The porch features a limestone foundation. The house's exterior walls are covered with clapboard.

10 John Heil House
159 North Main St. (Privately owned)

❖ This small c. 1860s painted German brick house is similar to the Firman A. Rozier office building on Merchant Street and the Pierre Schumert House at 73 North Main Street. In 2019, students from Southeast Missouri State University conducted an in-depth, hands-on survey of the house. One of the things they noted was the use of horsehair in the plaster of the front

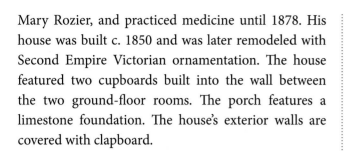

room attic, a practice common during the 19th century. The university has the state's only undergraduate historic preservation program certified by the National Council for Preservation Education.

11 Jean Ferdinand Rozier Store/ Francis Claude Rozier Building
193–195 North Main St. (Privately owned)

❖ French-born Jean Ferdinand Rozier arrived here in 1811 with fellow navy veteran John James Audubon. They planned to become merchants here as they had been in Louisville and Henderson, Kentucky. Audubon, however, was interested in ornithology and art. He left after six weeks, returning to Henderson where his wife still lived. He achieved fame as a celebrated bird artist, publishing his works in *The Birds of America*. Rozier remained and became a successful merchant,

later partnering with lead mogul Firmin Desloge. He erected the right half of the building in 1837. He had eight sons and two daughters. He and four sons served as Ste. Genevieve mayor. Three sons (Francis, Felix, and Firmin) married daughters of Jean Baptiste Valle Jr., thus combining with mining interests. Francis and Felix built mansions on adjoining North Main Street lots. Francis's house at the corner of Merchant and Main Streets was razed in 1960. His brother's home survives as Inn St. Gemme Bauvais/Felix Rozier House. This building dates to c. 1875.

12 Main St. Inn Bed & Breakfast/ Meyer's Hotel
221 North Main St. at Washington St. (Privately owned B&B)

❖ This two-story 1882 brick structure was built to provide lodging to weary Ste. Genevieve visitors and it continues to do so today. Mary Wehner Meyer, a widow with three small children, was the proprietor of this establishment, which was advertised in the May 17, 1890, issue of Ste. Genevieve's *Fair Play* newspaper. The ad boldly stated, "This Hotel is NEW, Roomy, and in every way Equal to any in Southeast Missouri. All accommodations are FIRST CLASS. Every attention will be rendered for the comfort and convenience of permanent or transient guests. First Class Sample Rooms for Commercial Travelers." Mary later added a bar structure to the main building. Attention to every detail continues today at Main Street Inn B&B.

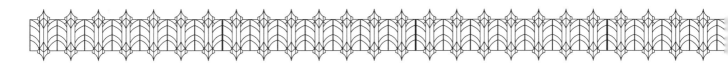

The building was first renovated and restored in 1990. After extensive renovations, the inn reopened in 2017 with 10 guest rooms, private baths, plenty of public spaces inside and out, and several ancient pecan trees.

13 Eloy LeCompte House
231 North Main St. (Private residence)

❖ This limestone house was constructed c. 1840. It was designed so the first floor sits above street level. Steps to reach the house were hidden behind a stone wall

COURTESY OF LIBRARY OF CONGRESS, PUBLIC DOMAIN

near the sidewalk. Eloy LeCompte was born across the Mississippi River in Prairie du Rocher (now Illinois). He married a Ste. Genevieve woman named Melanie Bogy and bought about 10 acres of land here. He had a stone grain mill, Cone Mill, built north of his house in about 1856.

14 Eloy LeCompte Mill/ Cone Mill/MFA Mill
305 North Main St. (Private residence)

❖ This c. 1856 building contained one of Ste. Genevieve's first steam-powered mills, Cone Mill. By 1880, Martin Meyer was a mill superintendent. He was

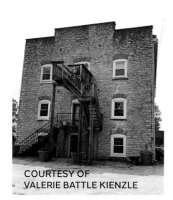

severely injured that year when an explosion at the mill blew up part of the structure's stone wall and equipment. Meyer later died and the mill was rebuilt. His widow, Mary, became proprietor of Meyer's Hotel, today's nearby Main Street Inn

COURTESY OF VALERIE BATTLE KIENZLE

Bed & Breakfast. An 1888 advertisement in the *Fair Play* stated: "The farming Community and the Public generally will bear in mind that the 'CONE MILLS' always pay the Highest Market Price for Wheat, and in Cash only. The well-known choice Brands of Flour, 'Cone' and 'Eloy,' and other grades kept continually on sale, at the lowest possible figures."

👣 Cross North Main Street. Note the tall pole near the North Main Street Bridge over the North Fork of the Gabouri Creek. It displays high-water marks for 20th-century Ste. Genevieve flood events. Floodwaters reached their highest level on August 6, 1993, at 49.74 feet. Continue walking on this side of North Main Street.

COURTESY OF VALERIE BATTLE KIENZLE

15 Bertha Doerge House
222 North Main St. (Private residence)

❖ This Second Empire brick house with a limestone foundation and arched windows was built c. 1880. It was the home of Charles and Bertha Straube Doerge, both born in Germany. Bertha's work was important in a small town at that time. In addition to having several children of her own, she was the local midwife, a trusted and experienced provider who helped many local women give birth. It is thought that Bertha helped deliver more than 1,000 babies.

COURTESY OF VALERIE BATTLE KIENZLE

16 Blacksmith's Shop
202 North Main St.

❖ This c. 1900 building once held a blacksmith shop. Blacksmiths played an important role in the daily lives of residents, forging and shaping everything from knives

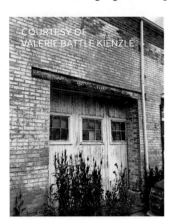

COURTESY OF VALERIE BATTLE KIENZLE

and utility tools to plows, carriage wheels, horseshoes, and door locks. Ste. Genevieve had several blacksmiths. The building has two flues for the blacksmith's forge. During the mid-20th century, the building was a vehicle service station.

17 Henry Wilder House
198 North Main St.

❖ This c. 1870 commercial building has a limestone foundation and is covered in clapboards. Heinrich Ludwig Weide came to Ste. Genevieve in the 1840s and

COURTESY OF VALERIE BATTLE KIENZLE

changed his name to Henry Wilder. He married Rosine Jokerst in 1843 and formed a company to transport sand from nearby lead mines for the local firm Janis and Vallé. Due to its high lead content, the sand was shipped to Pittsburgh, Pennsylvania, for use in making lead crystal. Later, Wilder became a grain dealer and road overseer, and was involved in civic activities. He was one of the petitioners for chartering the German Lutheran Evangelical Church in Ste. Genevieve in the 1860s.

COURTESY OF VALERIE BATTLE KIENZLE

18 Oberle Building/Joseph Oberle House
176 North Main St. (Private residence on the left side)

❖ This brick building is comprised of two structures built about 25 years apart, c. 1865 to 1890. Joseph and Bernadine Oberle were this building's first owners. Here in Joseph Oberle's 1870s meat market the Oberle Sausage was born. The market building joins the Joseph Oberle House. Oberle Meats, Inc., continues operations on Highway 32 in Ste. Genevieve with the sixth generation of Oberle family members. Products include a variety of smoked meats, German-style sausages, pork tenderloins, and cheeses. Generations of local residents have fond memories of stopping by the store and enjoying some of the delicious smoked meats. This property also includes a brick smokehouse in the rear.

19 Main Street Park
North Main and Jefferson Streets

❖ Think of this as a tiny pocket park tucked into a historic, scenic neighborhood. The park has seating,

COURTESY OF VALERIE BATTLE KIENZLE

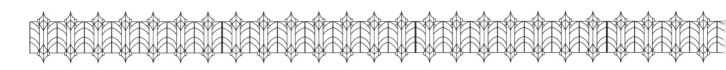

greenscaping, and restrooms. It's the perfect place to take a break from traversing the sidewalks and streets of this French-inspired city. After a brief rest, a walking tour of Ste. Genevieve can resume! The lot previously held a car wash and a commercial building.

COURTESY OF VALERIE BATTLE KIENZLE

20 Felix Rozier House/ The Inn St. Gemme Bauvais
78 North Main St. (Privately owned B&B)
❖ Felix Rozier was a son of Jean Ferdinand and Constance Roy Rozier. He was born in Ste. Genevieve and worked in Potosi, Perryville, and St. Marys before returning to marry Louise Valle, a daughter of Jean

COURTESY OF VALERIE BATTLE KIENZLE

Baptiste Valle Jr. He became one of the owners of the Valle Mining Company, served as mayor of Ste. Genevieve, and was the father of 11 children. The oldest portion of this brick house was constructed c. 1849, with later additions. The front yard features a low stone wall topped with wrought iron fencing. The property also contains an octagonal gazebo over a limestone French well. The house is listed in the National Register of Historic Places. Today, Rozier's mansion is a bed-and-breakfast inn.

21 Vital St. Gemme Bauvais House
20 South Main St. (Private residence)
❖ Joseph Vital St. Gemme Bauvais was born in Kaskaskia in 1738. He moved across the river to Ste. Genevieve and built the southern half of this French-style *poteaux-en-terre* house c. 1792. The northern half was built c. 1801. It is one of few such homes still in existence in the US and one of three in Ste. Genevieve.

The original vertical cedar log walls remain filled with *pierrotage*, a combination of stone and lime mortar. It has undergone multiple renovations. The most recent restoration's attention to historic detail earned it several awards, including the Ste. Genevieve Landmarks Award for Historical Preservation and the Preserve Missouri Award from the Missouri Preservation Society. Joseph's brother Jean Baptiste built Bauvais-Amoureux House.

👣 This is the end of Tour 1, the South Main Street and North Main Street Loop walk. To begin Tour 2, the Market Street and Merchant Street Loop walk, turn right onto Market Street at its intersection with South Main Street.

Did You Know?

❖ **The Mississippi River is the largest river system in North America.** It measures approximately 2,300 miles in length, beginning at Minnesota's Lake Itasca and flowing south to its delta at the Gulf of Mexico. It is considered the world's most economically important river system. Flooding has been a problem for Ste. Genevieve residents since its 18th-century founding. Significant flooding happened in 1785, 1844, 1942, 1943, 1944, 1947, 1951, 1973, 1982, 1993, and 1995. A tall pole on North Main Street displays watermark heights for 20th-century Ste. Genevieve flood events. Floodwater reached its highest level on August 6, 1993, at 49.74 feet.

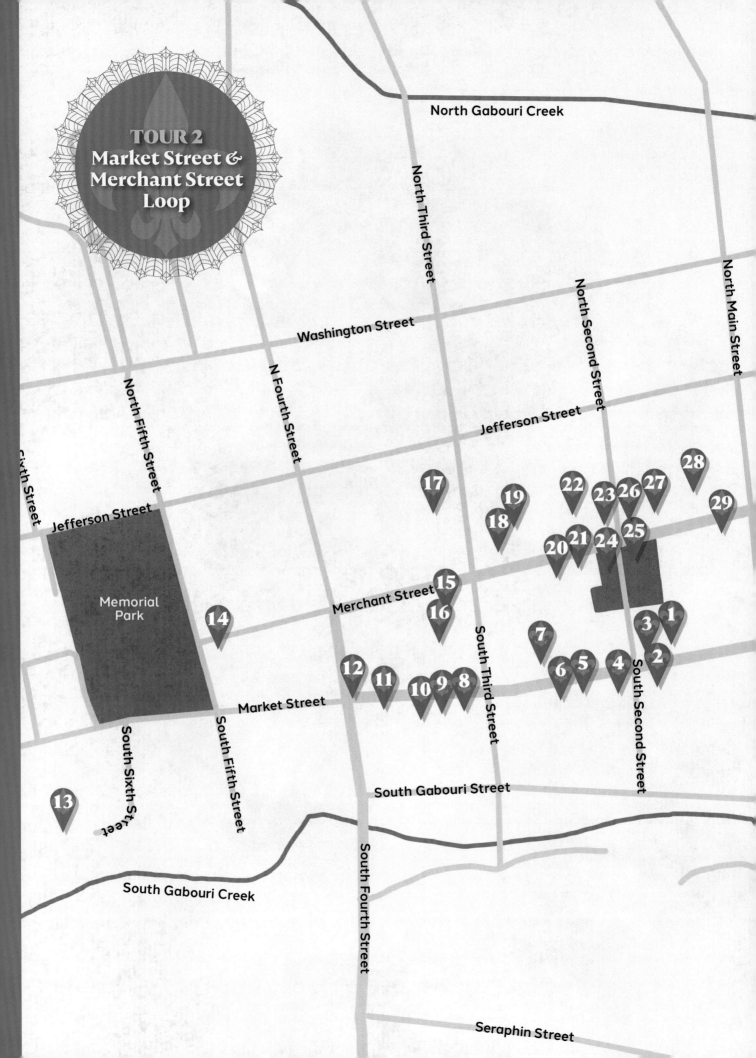

TOUR 2
Market Street & Merchant Street Loop

North Gabouri Creek

North Third Street

North Second Street

North Main Street

Washington Street

N Fourth Street

Jefferson Street

North Fifth Street

Sixth Street

Jefferson Street

Memorial Park

Merchant Street

South Third Street

South Second Street

Market Street

South Sixth Street

South Fifth Street

South Gabouri Street

South Fourth Street

South Gabouri Creek

Seraphin Street

TOUR 2
Market Street
& Merchant Street Loop
Approximately 1.1 miles

This walking tour begins at the intersection of Market and Main Streets, across from the Ste. Genevieve Welcome Center/Great River Road Welcome Center, 66 South Main Street. Park in the lot behind the Welcome Center off Market Street, or park along Market or Main Street. *(Note: Do not attempt to drive this route, as one-way driving applies on several streets. These directions are for **walking only**.)*

1 Ste. Genevieve Lions Club Park
155 Market St.

❖ Most days this is a quiet oasis in the middle of historic Ste. Genevieve, compliments of the local chapter of the International Lions Club, a community service organization. During citywide activities, it's

COURTESY OF VALERIE BATTLE KIENZLE

a hub for food and beverage purchases and outdoor dining. The historic marker tells an abbreviated version of the Ste. Genevieve story. This is a great place to read through literature from the Welcome Center or to take a walking break.

2 The Centre for French Colonial Life
198 Market St.

❖ The Centre for French Colonial Life in Ste. Genevieve has been open since 2017 and is operated by French Colonial America (FCA), a 501(c)(3) organization. It is the headquarters for the French Colonial America museum campus. The Centre features short- and

COURTESY OF VALERIE BATTLE KIENZLE

long-term historical exhibits and an education facility. Its museum campus includes four historic French Colonial properties—the Louis Bolduc House, the Bolduc-LeMeilleur House, the Bauvais-Linden House, and the François Vallé II House—plus its exhibits and education facility. These properties were owned by the National Society of the Colonial Dames of America in the State of Missouri until they were gifted to FCA in 2020. Fees are charged for property tours. Entry to the properties is through the Centre's main building.

3 Jean Baptiste Bossier House
195 Market St.

❖ This former home was built in several phases. The first phase was built by merchant Jean Baptiste Bossier c. 1818. Jean and his sister were born in Louisiana but moved to Ste. Genevieve as teens following the deaths of first their father and then their mother. Their mother was a member of the local St. Gemme Bauvais family. Jean married in

COURTESY OF VALERIE BATTLE KIENZLE

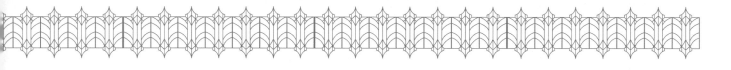

1808 and later made additions to this building, which was the location of his home. His business, the Jean Baptiste Bossier store and warehouse, was located at 200 Merchant Street (number 24 on this tour). Another addition was made c. 1890. Today, the building is occupied by a business.

4 Holy Cross Lutheran Church
200 Market St.

❖ Holy Cross was founded in the spring of 1867 by a group of German Lutherans who had moved to the Ste. Genevieve area. Services were held at a building on

COURTESY OF VALERIE BATTLE KIENZLE

Main Street until this c. 1869 brick Romanesque Revival church was completed. The building has a raised limestone foundation, a steep gable roof, and arched windows. Rev. Otto F. Voigt, the first pastor, opened a school at the church in 1871. It became known locally as the German School, and lessons were taught in both German and English. Services are still held there today. The education building at the rear dates to 1990.

5 Anthony Kempff Building/Kempff–Jaccard Building and Stanton Building
234 Market St.

❖ This commercial building was constructed with two differently styled storefronts, c. 1851 and 1860. It is thought to be the oldest commercial building on Market Street. F.A. Kempff had his jewelry

COURTESY OF VALERIE BATTLE KIENZLE

and watchmaking business in the left building. In 1912, Edward Stanton opened one of the area's first automobile dealerships and garages with a Ford Motors franchise. The building housed other enterprises during the 20th century until the 1980s. By then the building was in disrepair and slated for demolition. However, concerned citizens who valued the city's historic buildings were successful in campaigning against demolition. The building was spared and today houses another local business.

6 Marie Hubardeau LaPorte House
248 Market St. (Privately owned B&B)

❖ This c. 1830 timber-frame residence is representative of the community's 19th-century French residents embracing the Anglo-American building details favored at that time. The house has a center brick chimney but has been modified through the years.

COURTESY OF VALERIE BATTLE KIENZLE

Today the exterior has been covered with clapboard and a metal roof. Marie was the daughter of Simon Hubardeau Jr. and Genevieve Pancheron, who moved from French Canada and settled in the first area known as Ste. Genevieve.

7 John Ferguson Scott Marker
255 Market St.
(Ste. Genevieve County Bicentennial Plaza)

❖ The name John Ferguson Scott may not be familiar to many, but he played an important role in Ste. Genevieve and also the territory that became the state

of Missouri. He arrived in Ste. Genevieve to practice law after graduating from Princeton University in 1805. He was the first permanent lawyer in town. He was the Congressional Delegate of the Territory of Missouri from 1817 until 1821.

During that time, he petitioned Congress several times for Missouri's statehood. After statehood was achieved in 1821, he served as a member of the US House of Representatives from 1821 until 1827. He is buried in Ste. Genevieve Memorial Cemetery.

8 *Ste. Genevieve Herald*
316A Market St.

❖ Brick, a cast-iron front, and pressed metal highlight the exterior of this c. 1905 commercial building. The affixing of cast-iron fronts to commercial buildings was a popular way to update buildings around the turn of the 19th century. This building once was home to Rozier Store. Since 2021, part of the building is the home of the *Ste. Genevieve Herald*. The newspaper was first published on May 6, 1882. A German edition, *Ste. Genevieve Herold*, was published from May 13, 1882, until February 2, 1895.

A German-language page was included in the English edition from February 9, 1895, until March 30, 1918. It is the official legal weekly publication of Ste. Genevieve County and covers multiple area communities.

9 Ferdinand Roy Building/ *Ste. Genevieve Herald* Building
330 Market St. (Private)

❖ This c. 1865 commercial building was home to the *Ste. Genevieve Herald* newspaper for many decades. The newspaper's first issue was published on May 6,

1882, by editor Joseph A. Ernst. Today, the *Herald* continues as a weekly publication devoted to local news coverage of Ste. Genevieve County. It is the county's most widely distributed publication and also is available online. This building is not currently open to the public.

10 Ste. Genevieve Museum Learning Center/Koetting Building
360 Market St.

❖ Built in 1910 on the town square, the Koetting Building once housed a dry-goods store and grocery. After extensive renovations, the collections of the decades-old Sainte Genevieve Museum were moved into the multilevel building in 2018. Today, the Ste. Genevieve Museum Learning Center has displays focusing on paleontology, geology, archaeology, mining, wars, and history. The stated mission of the nonprofit Learning Center is "Preserving the Past for Future Generations." This multifaceted attraction features hundreds of artifacts, specimens, and collections of curator Guy Darrough, who made significant discoveries into what has become the official dinosaur of the state of Missouri, *Parrosaurus Missouriensis*.

11 Quarry Workers Local 829
380 Market St.

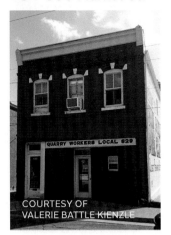

COURTESY OF VALERIE BATTLE KIENZLE

❖ Red brick and arched second-story windows with keystones highlight the front exterior of this c. 1894 building. The union was established in 1937. Generations of Ste. Geneviens have worked in the quarry industry and have been represented by this labor union. Local artist and businessperson Joy French has painted murals on several Ste. Genevieve buildings, including this one.

👣 Cross the street at the intersection of Market and Fourth Streets. Continue on Market Street.

12 Formerly Leon Vorst's Station
Corner of Market and Fourth Streets

❖ This c. 1928 building may not seem significant at first glance, but it is a remnant of a bygone era. During the mid-20th century, US-made automobiles flourished as more and more Americans hit the highways and byways in their own vehicles. And accompanying that trend was the need for service stations. Stations of that era did indeed provide service to drivers. Cars pulled into stations like this

COURTESY OF VALERIE BATTLE KIENZLE

one and triggered a ringing bell. Attendants then greeted drivers, pumped gas, cleaned windshields, and checked oil levels and tire pressure. These services were available at no extra charge with each gasoline purchase. Self-service gasoline pumps were nonexistent. If a car needed an oil change or to have tires rotated, drivers pulled into one of the large bays.

👣 Stay on Market Street to the rear boundary of Memorial Cemetery at the corner of Fifth and Market Streets.

13 Knights of Columbus Hall, Council 1037
600 Market St. (Only open to the public for special events and fundraisers)

❖ The impressive gate and mansion on the left are home to the Knights of Columbus fraternal benefit organization, but for many decades the building was a

COURTESY OF VALERIE BATTLE KIENZLE

private residence. Jules Petrequin was general manager and part owner of Western Lime Works when he built this large brick Colonial Revival house in 1912. He also was a director of the local Home Light and Water Company. This house was unlike any other Ste. Genevieve residence. It is the city's only Colonial Revival/ Beaux Arts mansion. Ownership of the home passed to Fred and Viola Oberle, who worked for the Petrequins, following Mrs. Petrequin's 1950 death. The Knights of Columbus organization purchased the house in 1959 and uses it as their meeting hall.

👣 To continue Tour 2, retrace your steps back to the intersection of Market and Fifth Streets by the cemetery. Turn left onto Fifth Street. Follow Fifth to the intersection with Merchant Street. Turn right onto Merchant.

COURTESY OF
VALERIE BATTLE KIENZLE

14 Dr. Walter Fenwick House
498 Merchant St. (Private residence)

❖ Cosmetic alterations have been made to this c. 1805 timber-frame, limestone-foundation house, but it still retains some of its original architectural details. Dr. Fenwick was a Kentucky physician who married Julia Vallé, a member of the prominent Vallé family, in 1801. He was one of Ste. Genevieve's first surgeons. He also served on the board of trustees for Ste. Genevieve Academy. On October 1, 1811, he fought a pistol duel with Kentucky lawyer Thomas T. Crittenden on Moreau's Island near Kaskaskia, Illinois. Fenwick was injured in the duel and died the next day. He is buried in nearby Ste. Genevieve Memorial Cemetery. Some believe the house is haunted.

COURTESY OF
VALERIE BATTLE KIENZLE

15 Sainte Genevieve Art Center and Art Museum
310 Merchant St.

❖ The Sainte Genevieve Art Center and Art Museum is an inclusive 501(c)(3) nonprofit community organization where regional artists can learn, share ideas, and display their work. The group hosts workshops throughout the year for people of all ages. The Sainte Genevieve Art Guild's goal is to promote creative expression and to preserve the history of amateur and professional visual artists in the area. Each year, it coordinates the Sainte Genevieve Plein Air Painting Competition and hosts exhibits of the works of local creatives at the Art Center and Art Museum. The guild's stone building on Courthouse Square was constructed in 1933 for the city's 1935 bicentennial celebration.

16 Island of Flags at the Courthouse Parking Lot
Merchant Street and Dubourg Place

COURTESY OF
VALERIE BATTLE KIENZLE

❖ Seventeen flags associated with Ste. Genevieve fly along the outside perimeter of the parking lot for the Ste. Genevieve County Courthouse. These include the Ste. Genevieve Municipal flag, the State of Missouri flag, and flags for the Fraternal Order of Eagles, the Rotary Club, 4-H Clubs, the American Legion, Veterans of Foreign Wars, the Girl Scouts, the Lions Club, the Elks Club, the Jaycees, the Foundation for Restoration of Ste. Genevieve, and the National Park Service. The American flag is at the center and is displayed on a taller flagpole than the others.

 Continue to follow Merchant Street.

17 Rozier's Store/Dubourg Centre
307 Merchant St. at Third St.

❖ This building was constructed in 1924 by Jokerst and Yealy, a mercantile company. It was sold to the Rozier Company in 1936. The Rozier family has been active in mercantile, merchandising, and retail establishments in Ste. Genevieve and Perry County for generations, dating back to the brief partnership between Jean Ferdinand Rozier and John James Audubon. Audubon left Ste. Genevieve and became a world-renowned artist; Rozier remained and became a successful businessman. The building faces Courthouse Square.

COURTESY OF
VALERIE BATTLE KIENZLE

18 Mary E. Kern Building/Myers Shoes
289 Merchant St.

❖ This c. 1893 commercial brick building with a limestone foundation has a well-preserved facade that features elaborate pressed-metal, cast-iron

COURTESY OF
VALERIE BATTLE KIENZLE

ornamentation. It is one of the best-preserved buildings of its type in the area. Use of decorative metal on buildings was extremely popular in the US in the late 19th century as a way to update the looks of commercial buildings. The metal on this building was forged by a St. Louis company, Mesker Brothers Iron Works. St. Louis had numerous such companies at that time. The current paint accents the facade's details and embellishments.

19 The Orris
265 Merchant St.

❖ Like many towns in the early decades of the 20th century, downtown Ste. Genevieve had a local movie house, the Orris Theater. Built in 1933 of unique mustard-colored bricks and named for a brand of flour milled in St. Mary, the theater has shown hundreds of movies

COURTESY OF
VALERIE BATTLE KIENZLE

through the years and has been the scene of numerous stage productions. It featured one of the area's first air-conditioning systems, using well water to provide cooling. The Orris Cafe opened next door in July 1934. Generations of locals spent many hours being entertained within its walls until 1975. Community theater groups then used the facility into the 1980s. After falling into disrepair, the building was sold, gutted, and reopened as a music performance venue. The building's marquee remains.

20 Rozier Outbuilding
242 Merchant St. (Private residence)

❖ The original, small, c. 1811 brick structure stands behind this c. 1910 house. The brick portion was an outbuilding of the Jean Ferdinand Rozier House. Rozier arrived in Ste. Genevieve in 1811 with fellow US Navy veteran John James Audubon. Their intent was to become successful merchants. Audubon, however, had a strong interest in ornithology and art. He left Ste. Genevieve within a year and achieved fame as a bird artist, publishing his many

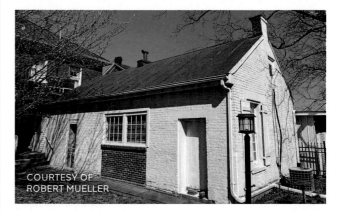

COURTESY OF
ROBERT MUELLER

works in a book, *The Birds of America*, released in sections between 1827 and 1838. Rozier remained and became a successful merchant. The bricks in the structure's oldest section are handmade, and the building retains many of its original wooden construction materials.

21 Emile P. Vogt House
234 Merchant St.

❖ Emile P. Vogt was born in 1842 in the small frame Theophilus Dufour House (220 Merchant Street) next door to his c. 1880 two-story brick house. The brick house still looks much like it did when he built it, with some original materials. Vogt worked as a land examiner for Ste. Genevieve and created numerous

COURTESY OF
VALERIE BATTLE KIENZLE

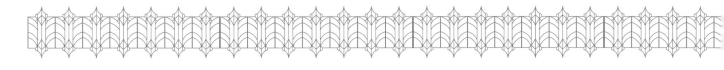

extensive property abstracts. He was active in the Catholic Church and enjoyed singing in the choir there. He died in 1897 and is buried in Valle Spring Cemetery.

COURTESY OF LIBRARY OF CONGRESS PUBLIC DOMAIN

22 Abraham Newfield House/ Senator Lewis F. Linn House
223 Merchant St. (Private residence)

❖ This c. 1806 central-chimney, limestone-block-foundation I-house has had multiple additions made to it through the years. Antoine Parfait Dufour was the original owner of this lot, and in 1808 he sold it to Abraham Newfield, who built the original part of the house. He sold it to Ferdinand Rozier in 1820. The house was sold to Dr. Lewis F. Linn in 1826. Dr. Linn, a contemporary of Missouri Senator Thomas Hart Benton, was a US senator from 1833 until 1843. He was instrumental in encouraging the settlement of the Pacific Northwest and in establishing a border between the Oregon Territory and Canada. He also was famous for the treatment of cholera. He died of an aneurysm in Ste. Genevieve. The State of Missouri erected a monument at his grave site describing him as a "model senator."

23 Dufour Stone Building/Rozier Bank
201 Merchant St. at Second St. (Private, not open to the public)

❖ This building's history dates to 1818. Early colonist Antoine Parfait Dufour was said to have owned the property before this unique, stone-block building was constructed by the firm Kiel, Bisch & Roberts. The building's front and rear feature ashlar stone; the sides are fieldstone. The building later was

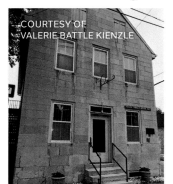

COURTESY OF VALERIE BATTLE KIENZLE

sold to local resident Dr. Lewis F. Linn, a US senator, in about 1831. Henry L. Rozier Sr. later purchased it to house a bank. It became the Rozier Bank in 1891 and operated under that name for many decades. The bank was robbed in 1939, and the city marshal was shot and injured. The robbers were caught and subsequently jailed. The building also housed the switchboards for the city's early telephone office. LeClere Janis was the wire master.

 Cross Merchant Street to 200 Merchant and Second Streets.

24 Jean Baptiste Bossier Warehouse/ Dr. Benjamin Shaw House/ Mammy Shaw House
200 Merchant St. at Second St.

❖ This lot was acquired by Antoine Parfait Dufour, an Old Town Ste. Genevieve resident, in 1793. He sold it to Jean Baptiste Bossier in 1818, who had the original section of this building constructed as a storehouse for his mercantile business. Physician Dr. Benjamin Shaw bought the property in 1837. He made additions and used it as his residence. After his death, his widow, Emilie Janis LeCompte Shaw, a daughter of former Green Tree Tavern owner François Janis, lived there until 1897. The famous Ste. Genevieve Art Colony and school organized in the 1930s was headquartered here.

Dr. Benjamin Shaw
COURTESY OF MISSOURI HISTORICAL SOCIETY, ST. LOUIS

COURTESY OF VALERIE BATTLE KIENZLE

Today, the restored building is part of the Felix Valle House State Historic Site in the Ste. Genevieve National Historic Landmark District. The house retains many original construction components.

Ste. Genevieve Art Colony

❖ Ste. Genevieve Art Colony was founded in 1932 by two St. Louis artists. Beginning in 1934, the Ste. Genevieve Summer School of Art was held for several years. Rather than painting still-life pieces, the artists captured the sometimes harsh and gritty realities of workers and people living through the Great Depression.

COURTESY OF
LIBRARY OF CONGRESS,
PUBLIC DOMAIN

STE. GENEVIEVE
SUMMER SCHOOL
OF ART

COURTESY OF
MISSOURI HISTORICAL
SOCIETY, ST. LOUIS

Instructors included famed Missouri artists Thomas Hart Benton and Aimee Schweig. The artists were headquartered at the Jean Baptiste Bossier Warehouse/Dr. Benjamin Shaw House/Mammy Shaw House, 200 Merchant and Second Streets. A display of selected pieces can be seen in the stone building behind the house. The school attracted visitors from outside the community, which may have contributed to the city becoming a tourist destination. Colony participant Martyl Schweig painted the mural, *La Guignolée*, inside the local post office.

25 Felix Valle House State Historic Site/Jacob Philipson House

198 Merchant St. at Second St.

❖ This American-Federal style native ashlar stone house was built by Jacob Philipson in 1818 as a residence and mercantile store. Its style varied from the many French-influenced homes in Ste. Genevieve. Felix (grandson of

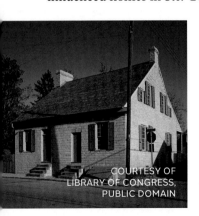
COURTESY OF
LIBRARY OF CONGRESS,
PUBLIC DOMAIN

François Valle I) and Odile Pratte Valle, members of two of Ste. Genevieve's premier Colonial families, purchased the home in 1824. They lived here and ran the Menard & Vallé trading business from here. The house is furnished with c. 1830s furniture and accessories. The property also features a garden and several outbuildings. It is a State Historic Site and is managed by the Missouri Department of Natural Resources. Guided tours of the site are available for a fee. Events and programs focusing on French customs are held throughout the year.

26 Jesse B. Robbins House

199 Merchant St. (Private residence)

❖ Born in 1818, Jesse Robbins was the son of Prospect K. Robbins (1782–1847). Prospect was an early land surveyor who was contracted by the US General Land Office to survey the first 375 miles of the Fifth Principal Meridian in the United States, the north–south line from

COURTESY OF
VALERIE BATTLE KIENZLE

which all land surveys are based in Missouri and five other states. Jesse became a lawyer and served in the Missouri Legislature in 1850. He built this impressive c. 1860s Italianate brick house and lived here until his death in 1879. After major renovation work in more recent years, it is listed in the National Register of Historic Places.

27 Joseph Bogy House/ Bogy-Bussen House

163 Merchant St. (Private residence)

❖ A portion of this house was built of logs c. 1810 by Joseph Bogy. He was part owner of a lead mine and ran a store in Ste. Genevieve. He served in both the Missouri House of Representatives and the Senate. His son Lewis V. Bogy became an acting US Commissioner of Indian Affairs and served in the US Senate from 1873–1877.

COURTESY OF
VALERIE BATTLE KIENZLE

He also served in the state House of Representatives. The original Bogy House was torn down in 1873 and the current house was built. It retains some of the hewn logs and floor joists from the original house. The Bussen family members were great benefactors to Ste. Genevieve. Their estate provided the monies to build the community center on Highway 32.

 US Post Office
135 Merchant St.

❖ This building was constructed in 1939 with US Treasury Department funds and remains in service. The post office also contains a 1942 mural painted by American postwar and contemporary painter Martyl Schweig. An alumnus of Washington University in St. Louis, she had attended painting classes at the Ste. Genevieve Art Colony with her mother, Aimee Schweig, one of the colony's founders.

The mural depicts *La Guignolée*, a Ste. Genevieve New Year's Eve tradition that dates to the area's 18th-century founding. Local residents don costumes and gather in homes and taverns to sing and dance in what has been described as perhaps the oldest continual European-origin tradition celebrated in Missouri.

 Firman A. Rozier Building
124 Merchant St.

❖ This small c. 1850 single-story brick building was used by General Firman Andrew Rozier as an office. Rozier, one of eight sons and two daughters of Ferdinand Rozier, was of French descent, but he made use of the fine brickwork skills of some of the German craftsmen who moved to the area in the mid-19th century. This building is structurally similar to the John Heil (Hael) House and the Pierre Schumert House on Main Street.

Rozier was a lawyer and president of Ste. Genevieve Saving Association, raised troops for the Mexican–American War, served as the city's mayor, and was elected to both the Missouri House of Representatives and Senate. He and his wife, Mary M. Valle, were the parents of seven children.

👣 This is the end of Tour 2, the Market Street and Merchant Street Loop walk. To return to your vehicle, follow Merchant Street to its intersection with South Main Street. Turn right onto South Main and continue back to the Welcome Center parking area.

Did You Know?

❖ **Ste. Genevieve commerce in the early 1800s consisted mainly of agriculture, furs/peltries, and lead.** Any of these could be used as money or exchange. At that time, keelboats were the only means of transportation by water. The first steamboat, *General Pike*, arrived in Ste. Genevieve on August 1, 1817, with much celebration. Several more steamboats arrived through the years, but regular steamboat navigation did not begin there until 1824.

❖ **The Great River Road,** a National Scenic Byway and All-American Road, follows the Mississippi River for approximately 3,000 miles, from Minnesota to Louisiana. It runs through Missouri from Hannibal to New Madrid and the state's Bootheel. It passes through Ste. Genevieve near the Modoc River Ferry landing.

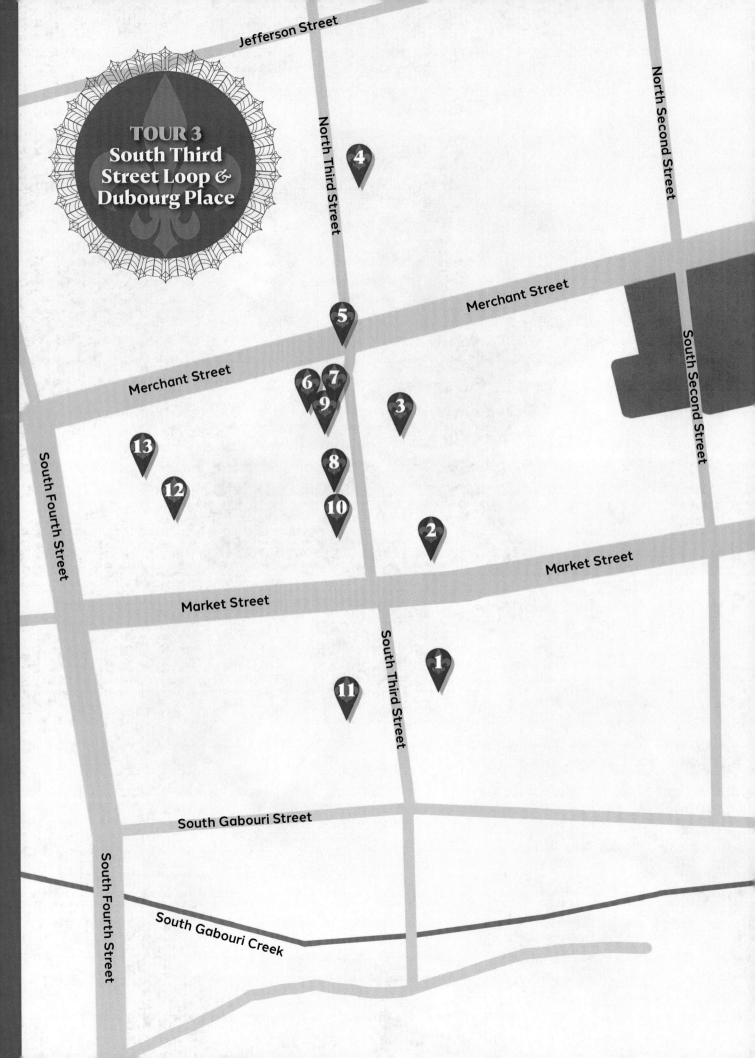

TOUR 3
South Third Street Loop & Dubourg Place
Approximately 0.4 miles

✦ This walking tour begins on South Third Street near the Southern Hotel, 146 South Third Street. Look for street parking.

1 Southern Hotel/John Donahue House
150 South Third St. (Private residence)

❖ This imposing Federal-style brick structure dates to the early 1800s. It was built as a residence for John Donahue. Joseph Vorst bought the building before the Civil War and opened it as the Southern Hotel. He placed an advertisement in the January 21, 1888, edition of *Fair Play* newspaper stating, ". . . the best Accommodations of any Hotel in Southeast Missouri. The traveling Public

COURTESY OF VALERIE BATTLE KIENZLE

will find here an excellent table, good rooms, and the most courteous attention. For commercial travelers, I have a handsome and commodious Sample Room." Numerous renovations and additions have been made to the building through the years. It most recently operated as the Southern Hotel Bed & Breakfast.

2 Old Brick House/John Price House
90 South Third St. at Market St.

❖ A marker on this building says it was the first brick house constructed west of the Mississippi River. The Federal-style building was constructed of handmade bricks c. 1804–1806 for merchant and ferry operator

COURTESY OF VALERIE BATTLE KIENZLE

John Price, who ran a ferry between Ste. Genevieve and Kaskaskia, Illinois. Some question this construction date, saying it could have been built in 1780, 1790, or in the early 1800s. The first American district court was said to have been held on this site. The building also served as a territorial courthouse and a school from 1824 until 1842. The front room contains an original Bucks Gem-No. 36 woodstove used continuously from about 1856 until 1956. Once a tavern, the building houses a restaurant today.

3 The Anvil Restaurant & Saloon
46 South Third St.

❖ This commercial building housed a hardware store during the 1850s. It then became a saloon and adjoining barbershop. It is considered to be one of the city square's oldest buildings. It still contains many

COURTESY OF VALERIE BATTLE KIENZLE

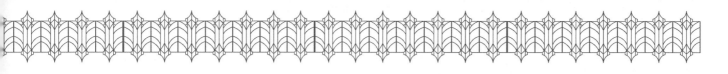

original architectural elements popular in buildings of that era, including decorative brickwork, original doors and doorjambs, maple floors, the bar and back bar, a pressed metal ceiling, and a pressed metal storefront. The bar was transported here by wagon from an 1850s steamboat that was stuck on a sandbar. An exposed exterior wall features a painted advertisement for Selz Royal Blue Shoes. Selz Shoes were made in the early 20th century by German immigrant Rolf Selz. Ghost signs of this ad can be found on brick buildings in cities throughout the US.

4 Martin Intress House
52 North Third St. (Privately owned B&B)

❖ This small German brick house was built c. 1842 to 1846. It is thought to be the oldest surviving German vernacular structure in Ste. Genevieve. It has a rubble

COURTESY OF VALERIE BATTLE KIENZLE

stone foundation and a wood-framed ell extending from the rear of the house. It is distinctly different from the traditional French-inspired architecture found on so many buildings in the city. It is a part of the Ste. Genevieve Historic District.

👣 Cross North Third Street and circle back.

5 Rozier's/Dubourg Centre
301 Merchant St. at Third St.

❖ This building is included on Tour 2, but approaching it from this direction, note the Rozier's ghost sign and the use of decorative mural painting on one of the building's long Third Street walls. The mural

Mural at 301 Merchant at Third Streets, designed and painted by Kenzie Wolk
COURTESY OF VALERIE BATTLE KIENZLE

The Great Egret by Kenzie Wolk celebrates Ste. Genevieve's 250th anniversary. The Rozier family has been active in mercantile, merchandising, and retail establishments in Ste. Genevieve and Perry County for generations. This building opened in 1924 as the Jokerst and Yearly mercantile store. With its detailed brickwork, it is a good example of early-20th-century architecture. The building faces Courthouse Square.

6 Ste. Genevieve Chamber of Commerce
51 South Third St.

❖ This small, single-story red brick government building was constructed in 1875 as the Fireproof Clerk's Building. It is one of two similar public buildings located on Ste. Genevieve's Public Square. The building has a limestone foundation and ornamentation and rounded windows. Today, it houses offices for the

COURTESY OF VALERIE BATTLE KIENZLE

Ste. Genevieve Chamber of Commerce. The chamber's stated mission is "to serve as an umbrella organization, striving to promote local businesses, arts and education while improving the quality of life by maintaining and developing the economic and historic environment of Ste. Genevieve and the surrounding area."

7 *El Camino Real* Marker
Near 51 South Third St. (East side of the Courthouse)

❖ During the Colonial era, *El Camino Real* was a roadway that ran along the Mississippi River and connected the cities of New Madrid, Cape Girardeau, Ste. Genevieve, and St. Louis. It is considered one of the oldest roadways in Missouri and was used by the Spanish

COURTESY OF VALERIE BATTLE KIENZLE

(who gave it the name *El Camino Real*), the French (who called it *Rue Royale*), and Native Americans. Roughly translated, it means "The Royal Road," "The King's Way," or "Kings Highway." The commemorative marker was placed here in 1917 by the Missouri Daughters of the American Revolution. They placed similar markers in Kimmswick and Perryville, as well as in Cape Girardeau and New Madrid. Markers also exist in Caruthersville, Sikeston, Benton, and Rock Levee in Scott County. Ste. Genevieve's marker is located between the side of the Ste. Genevieve Courthouse and the Ste. Genevieve Area Chamber of Commerce building.

8 Old Ste. Genevieve County Courthouse
55 South Third St.

❖ Ste. Genevieve is the primary city and the county seat of Ste. Genevieve County, Missouri. Early courts in the county met in homes until a tax levy paid for construction of a building in the 1820s. This brick Eastlake-style public building with sandstone trim was constructed on the foundation of the previous courthouse and was

COURTESY OF MISSOURI HISTORICAL SOCIETY, ST. LOUIS

completed in 1886. St. Louis architect Jerome B. Legg designed this building, as well as similar courthouse buildings in St. Charles, Gasconade, Shelby, and St. François Counties. The south addition was completed in 1985. An original elevation drawing of the building is displayed inside.

9 *Milice de Ste. Genevieve* Marker, Battle of Fort San Carlos
51 South Third St.

❖ Ste. Genevieve played a role in the Revolutionary War. Spain entered the war against Great Britain in July 1779. The British wanted to control the Mississippi River valley, starting with St. Louis and Cahokia, Illinois. Spain heard about the planned attack on St. Louis, built a stone fortification tower called Fort San Carlos, and dug defense

COURTESY OF VALERIE BATTLE KIENZLE

trenches. Spain feared it would be outnumbered in a conflict with the British, plus Canadians and Native Americans supported the British. Spain asked Ste. Genevieve for help. A small garrison of regular soldiers and 60 militia (called *Milice de Ste. Genevieve*) arrived in St. Louis. When the attacking British

arrived in St. Louis on May 26, 1780, they realized they could not penetrate the local defenses, so they withdrew back to British territory. This event has been called the Battle of Fort San Carlos and is commemorated with a marker in front of the Ste. Genevieve Area Chamber of Commerce building.

COURTESY OF VALERIE BATTLE KIENZLE

10 Former Ste. Genevieve County Jail
51 South Third St.

❖ This brick Italianate government jail building (sometimes referred to by locals as the *calaboose*, a derivative of the Spanish word *calabozo*, or dungeon), was constructed in 1875 and is similar to the Fireproof Clerk/Chamber of Commerce building at 51 South Third Street (number 6 on this tour). It has a limestone block foundation and a wooden shingle roof. Barred windows once hinted at the building's former purpose. This building now houses the Ste. Genevieve County Prosecutor's Office.

 Cross Market Street and continue on South Third Street.

11 Thomure Icehouse
(Located behind ASL Pewter)
181 South Third St. (Rear, behind private residence)

❖ This c. 1800 building was built partially underground by J.B. Thomure using 20-inch-thick limestone. It is located behind today's ASL Pewter, but it once had an important purpose. Until the advent of electric

22 · Ste. Genevieve, Missouri

COURTESY OF VALERIE BATTLE KIENZLE

refrigeration, people needing to keep food cool built shelters over natural springs, lowering food containers into the frigid water, or they built icehouses. River communities made use of winter's frozen water. Special tools were used to cut and harvest ice into 50- to 100-pound blocks. Blocks were transported from the Mississippi River by wagons, packed in layers of straw or sawdust, and stored in icehouses. During frigid winters, enough ice was harvested and stored to last until the spring. Thomure Icehouse's stonework is similar to that of Hubardeau Icehouse off Jefferson Street.

Retrace your steps to the intersection of Market and Third Streets. Go left onto Market Street. Follow Market a short distance to its intersection with Dubourg Place. Turn right.

12 Old Valle School
61 Dubourg Pl.

❖ This limestone educational building was constructed in two parts. The right part, which is constructed of different stone, was built in 1873. The local pastor, Father Francis Weiss, had it built to be used as a Christian Brothers college. When teachers could not be found, he began using it as a rectory. The left half of the building was constructed in 1937 to house Valle's High

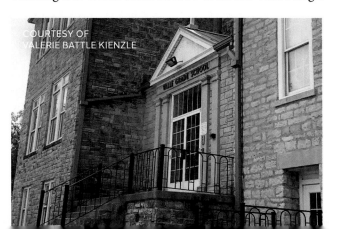

COURTESY OF VALERIE BATTLE KIENZLE

School. Earlier town schools of higher education were the Louisiana Academy (1808) and the Ste. Genevieve public high school (1913).

13 Ste. Genevieve Catholic Church
49 Dubourg Pl.

❖ Ste. Genevieve Parish is the oldest listed parish in what is now the Archdiocese of St. Louis and is the oldest in what is now the State of Missouri. It began keeping records in 1759. In 1794, the church that was located in *Le Grand Champ* southwest of the city's present location, was relocated to higher ground. Work began on a stone church in 1831, with a larger brick structure built around

Ste. Genevieve Catholic Church in the 1800s
COURTESY OF MISSOURI HISTORICAL SOCIETY, ST. LOUIS

COURTESY OF VALERIE BATTLE KIENZLE

it in 1876. It was enlarged to its current size in 1911. The church's spire and bell tower rise 190 feet above the city as they have since the 1870s and contain four bells. The largest is named Mary, followed by Genevieve, Francis, and Joseph. The first three were cast in St. Louis in 1906. The smallest, cast in Pittsburgh in 1847, is the "death bell" and rings when a parishioner dies.

👣 This is the end of Tour 3, the Third Street and Dubourg Place walk. To begin Tour 4, the St. Marys Road and South Gabouri Street walk, travel to and park near the intersection of South Main and South Gabouri Streets.

Did You Know?

❖ **By the fourth quarter of the 19th century,** Ste. Genevieve had dry-goods stores, groceries, a bank, cobblers, a tin shop, a tailor, a dressmaker, a jeweler and watchmaker, an attorney, stables, a livery and feed store, a lumberyard, a furniture store, various doctors, meat markets, a blacksmith, an undertaker, a barber, a surveyor, several restaurants, saloons and a dance hall, a public school, a courthouse and jail, hotels, and a Catholic church—the center of the city's activities.

❖ The Louisiana Territory included in 1803's Louisiana Purchase was under French rule, then under Spanish rule for 38 years, and again under French rule beginning in 1800. **The US government first flew a flag over Ste. Genevieve on March 10, 1804.**

❖ In the early days, salt was an important local commodity. **Ste. Genevieve's chief agricultural product was wheat, followed by corn/maize, tobacco, oats, hemp, and hops.** Flour exports to New Orleans were important to the city's economy. Flour also was shipped to St. Louis, New Madrid, and Cape Girardeau.

❖ **An execution by hanging was held in Ste. Genevieve on February 26, 1937.** The hundreds of people from throughout the state who gathered near the gallows to witness the hanging were an embarrassment to local citizens.

❖ **Ste. Genevieve is home to a producer of pure maple syrup.** River Aux Vases Pure Maple Syrup finished the 2022 maple syrup season with 100 gallons of the natural sweetener.

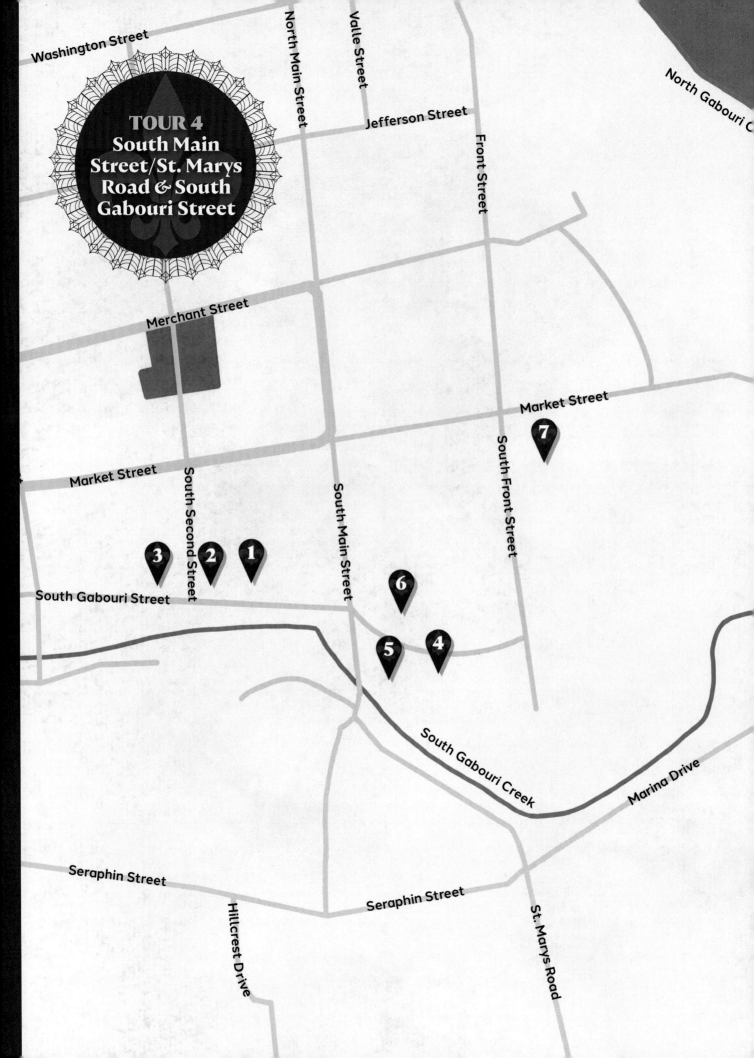

TOUR 4
South Main Street/St. Marys Road & South Gabouri Street

Washington Street

North Main Street

Valle Street

Jefferson Street

Front Street

North Gabouri C

Merchant Street

Market Street

Market Street

South Second Street

South Main Street

South Front Street

7

3 **2** **1**

South Gabouri Street

6

5 **4**

South Gabouri Creek

Marina Drive

Seraphin Street

Hillcrest Drive

Seraphin Street

St. Marys Road

TOUR 4
South Main Street/St. Marys Road & South Gabouri Street
Approximately 0.5 miles

✦ This walking tour begins where South Main Street becomes St. Marys Road *(near the railroad overpass bridge)* and its intersection with South Gabouri Street. Park on South Main. Turn right onto South Gabouri.

1 François Vallé II House
167 South Gabouri St. (Not currently open to the public)

❖ Although the exterior walls of this house are covered with clapboard and more recent ornamentation has been added, underneath are traditional French Colonial vertical *poteaux-sur-sol* log walls. François Vallé II was one of the four sons of the early Ste. Genevieve resident known as François Vallé I. Prior to building this house in the late 1700s on property owned by his father, he lived in the low-lying, flood-prone site first called Ste. Genevieve. He, along with many others residing in the area, grew tired of the constant threat of floods and relocated the town several miles inland from the Mississippi River. The house is located within the Ste. Genevieve Historic District. An archaeological excavation was conducted on the property in 2016.

COURTESY OF VALERIE BATTLE KIENZLE

2 Offices of the Foundation for Restoration of Ste. Genevieve & Mecker Research Library/Kiel-Schwent House
198 South Second St. at South Gabouri St.

❖ Henry Kiel was an important early-19th-century merchant who built this house c. 1813 and owned the lot until 1842. The house still contains some original materials, but renovations have been made and more recent items incorporated. The Kiel-Schwent building was donated to the Foundation for Restoration of Ste. Genevieve by Glennon and Rose Marie Schwent in 1994. Thomas Weil donated monies for the establishment of the Mecker Research Library to provide a central location for materials about historic Ste. Genevieve. The library is named for Bob and Odile Mecker, patrons of the Foundation for Restoration of Ste. Genevieve and the library. The library does not have regular hours but is open by appointment.

3 Sebastian Butcher House
229 South Gabouri St. (Private residence)

❖ German stonemason Sebastian Butcher bought the lot for this house in 1818 from the heirs of Marie Carpentier Vallé, widow of François Vallé II. Butcher's stonework is featured on several local historic houses, including the

COURTESY OF VALERIE BATTLE KIENZLE

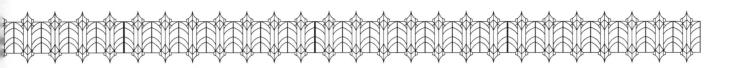

Simon Hubardeau Jr. House on Fourth Street. Deeds indicate that local resident Henry Kiel's printing office was at one time housed here. The house is part of the National Historic Landmark District in Ste. Genevieve.

👣 Retrace your steps on South Gabouri Street. Cross Main Street and walk under the railroad bridge to continue on South Gabouri.

4 Moses Austin Outbuilding
68 South Gabouri St. (Not open to the public)

❖ Moses Austin arrived in Upper Louisiana in the late 1790s with the idea of increasing lead production by introducing a different type of furnace. Spanish officials controlled the Upper Louisiana land at that time and granted Austin a concession on about 4,200 acres.

By 1799, Moses Austin's company was manufacturing 100,000 to 200,000 pounds of lead and shot annually. He and Col. Sam Hammond went on to cofound the nearby town of Herculaneum in 1809. Austin bought the land in these two parcels in 1798 from Amable Partnais *dit** Mason. He built a house and outbuildings, but the house was destroyed by fire. This c. 1810 structure was most likely one of the outbuildings built near the larger house.

Moses Austin
COURTESY OF STATE HISTORICAL SOCIETY OF MISSOURI

The word dit *(pronounced "dee" in French, translates as "called") used in a name was a common French Canadian custom.*

COURTESY OF VALERIE BATTLE KIENZLE

5 Moses Austin Outbuilding
72 South Gabouri St. (Not open to the public)

❖ This is the second parcel of land Moses Austin bought in 1798 from Amable Partnais *dit* Mason. The c. 1810 structure is thought to be another of Moses Austin's outbuildings once located near his home. He only lived on the property a short time, selling it in 1811. Austin, Texas, was named for his son, Stephen F. Austin. The two outbuildings are owned by the Jour de Fete's Day of Celebration organization.

6 Ratte *dit* Labruyere/Hoffman House
93 South Gabouri St.

❖ This beautifully restored and renovated house is said to have belonged to Louis Julian Ratte *dit* Labruyere,

who was one of the early settlers of the New Town site. His name first appears in a 1788 document. He and his wife, Marie Robert, had 17 children. He sold the property to American John McArthur in 1809, who probably built this house. Records indicate that lawyer and Territory of Missouri representative John Ferguson Scott once lived here. His contributions to the area are recognized on a plaque near the Ste. Genevieve Courthouse in the Ste. Genevieve County

A display at the Antique Mall (below left), and a locally made bar
COURTESY OF
VALERIE BATTLE KIENZLE

COURTESY OF
VALERIE BATTLE KIENZLE

Bicentennial Plaza. Until its restoration, this house was in a state of deterioration and disrepair. At one time, multiple rusted-out and junk vehicles littered the yard surrounding the house.

👣 Continue on South Gabouri Street. Turn left at the stop sign where it intersects with South Front Street. Continue on South Front until arriving at the entrance to the Antique Mall Ste. Genevieve, the long industrial building on the right.

7. The Antique Mall Ste. Genevieve/ Elder Manufacturing Company
Front and Market Streets

❖ This circa 1921 brick industrial building was constructed adjacent to the area's railroad tracks. During its 100-plus years of use, it has been used for the manufacture of washing machines, boilers, and shirts for St. Louis–based Elder Manufacturing Company. In the late 1920s, it housed the Ste. Genevieve Animal Manufacturing Co., which made aluminum tricycles in the shape of a pony. In the 1930s, Elder Manufacturing employed hundreds of local women. After years of

neglect, the building has been revitalized and now houses the Antique Mall Ste. Genevieve, a place where dozens of antique vendors can display and sell their wares. An interesting addition to the mall is a large, locally crafted wooden bar and beverage section, perfect for shopping breaks while hunting for treasures.

👣 This is the end of Tour 4, the St. Marys Road and South Gabouri Street walk. To return to your vehicle, turn left onto Market Street and cross the railroad tracks to continue to the intersection of Market and South Main Streets.

Did You Know?

❖ **Plank roads** were popular during the 19th century. Built between 1851 and 1853, the Ste. Genevieve, Iron Mountain, and Pilot Knob Plank Road was the longest in Missouri, measuring 42 miles long. It roughly followed Market Street, through Mississippi Lime Co., along Lime Kiln Road and Highway 32 to Farmington and beyond to Iron Mountain. It was built to haul iron ore and products to Ste. Genevieve for shipment on the Mississippi River. The road maintained its transportation importance until 1859 and the completion of the Iron Mountain Railroad, which diverted shipments to St. Louis. In addition, the road was expensive to maintain. An original section of the road is marked on Lime Kiln Road off Highway 61.

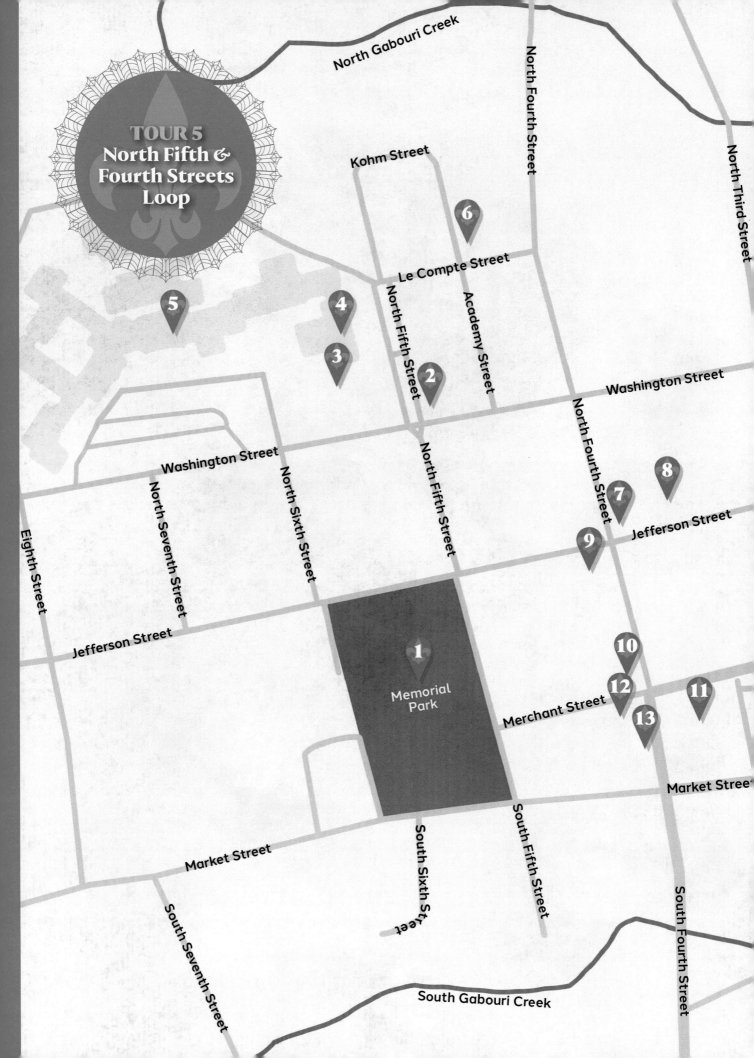

TOUR 5
North Fifth &
Fourth Streets
Loop

North Gabouri Creek

North Fourth Street

North Third Street

Kohm Street

Le Compte Street

6

Academy Street

5

4

North Fifth Street

3

2

Washington Street

North Fourth Street

8

7

Washington Street

North Seventh Street

North Sixth Street

North Fifth Street

9

Jefferson Street

Eighth Street

Jefferson Street

1

Memorial
Park

10

12

11

Merchant Street

13

Market Street

South Sixth Street

South Fifth Street

South Fourth Street

Market Street

South Seventh Street

South Gabouri Creek

This walking tour begins at the corner of North Fifth and Market Streets. *(Note: Do not attempt to drive this route, as one-way driving applies on several streets. These directions are for walking only.)*

1 Ste. Genevieve Memorial Cemetery/ Old Burying Ground

35 North Fifth St.

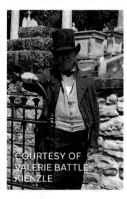

COURTESY OF VALERIE BATTLE KIENZLE

❖ Established in the late 1780s, this became the communal cemetery at the New Town location. It became the final resting place for people of all ages, races, and religions. It is divided into three sections and contains the remains of 3,500–5,000 people. The count is uncertain due to deterioration over time of many early wooden markers. Numerous people important to early Ste. Genevieve history are buried here. After the cemetery officially closed to new burials, burials were held in other local cemeteries, including Valle Spring Cemetery for Catholics, Crestlawn Cemetery, and the Lutheran Cemetery. The cemetery is managed by the nonprofit Foundation for Restoration of Ste. Genevieve and was added to the National Register of Historic Places in 1969.

Continue on North Fifth Street beyond the cemetery.

2 Auguste Aubuchon House

467 Washington St. at North Fifth St. (Private residence)

❖ This c. 1808 building is another example of French vertical log house construction on a raised limestone block foundation. Although it is covered in clapboards, it retains many of its original building materials. The house originally contained two rooms, one slightly larger than the other. The original central chimney, also made of limestone, divided the rooms. Auguste Aubuchon was born in 1774 to a family that could trace its lineage to Normandie, France. His extended family moved from there to Montreal, Canada, and then to Kaskaskia in what became the state of Illinois before settling in Ste. Genevieve.

COURTESY OF VALERIE BATTLE KIENZLE

3 Old Louisiana Academy/ The Academy/Sainte Genevieve Academy/Rozier Academy

201 North Fifth St. (Private residence)

❖ This ashlar stone building's date stone reads 1808. Located on Academy Hill above Fifth and Washington Streets, it offers a panoramic view of Ste. Genevieve. The school was organized in fall 1807 by subscribers who wanted to educate area children. Classes began in 1810. The first teacher had a heavy course load, including English, Latin, Greek, French, mathematics, arithmetic, logic, surveying, metaphysics, geography, history, and natural and moral philosophy. The Christian Brothers operated the academy from 1819 to 1822. It closed for a while. Firman Andrew Rozier purchased the building in 1853 and reopened the school. The school closed again during the Civil War. The Rozier family maintained the building as their residence. The property was sold to the Ste. Genevieve Board of Education in 1934. It sold again in 1994 and was restored.

The Academy, handbill, 1854
COURTESY OF MISSOURI HISTORICAL SOCIETY, ST. LOUIS

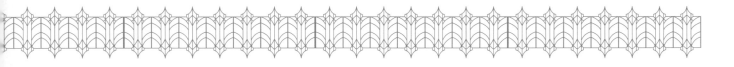

4 Ste. Genevieve Middle School
211 North Fifth St.

❖ This detailed building sits on a hill adjacent to the Old Louisiana Academy. It was designed by the St. Louis firm Bonsack and Pearce and completed in 1936

COURTESY OF
VALERIE BATTLE KIENZLE

in conjunction with the Works Progress Administration (WPA) to house Ste. Genevieve High School. This company also designed churches, schools, and civic buildings in other parts of Missouri. High school classes continued to be held here until the 1960s, when a new high school building was completed nearby. Additions and renovations have been made to the building. Middle school classes are held here now.

5 Ste. Genevieve High School
715 Washington St. *and*

Ste. Genevieve Elementary School
725 Washington St.

❖ This large complex of buildings includes the high school (Home of the Dragons), the elementary school (which serves children in pre-kindergarten through grade 5), and various athletic playing fields. All are part of the Ste. Genevieve R-II School District.

👣 *Return to Fifth Street where it branches with Washington Street. Cross Fifth Street and walk a short distance to its intersection with LeCompte Street. Travel on LeCompte for a short distance.*

6 Joseph Govreau House
451 LeCompte St. (Private residence)

❖ This c. 1800–1825 house is wrapped in aluminum siding, but underneath it is French vertical log construction. It has had several additions, but the

COURTESY OF
VALERIE BATTLE KIENZLE

original cellar still has cedar puncheons and a hand-hewn sill. At one time it had a barrel-vaulted brick enclosure in one cellar wall.

The house sits on land that was conveyed to Joseph Govreau in 1790. He was the brother of Etienne Joseph Govreau, whose house is located at 415 LaHaye Street. They were the sons of Dean Etienne Govreau and Marie Jeanne LaValley.

👣 *Circle back on LeCompte and resume walking on North Fifth Street. Turn left onto Jefferson Street. Continue briefly on Jefferson to see the Icehouse, and then circle back on Jefferson to Fourth Street. Turn left on Fourth Street and continue Tour 5.*

7 Jean Baptiste Hubardeau House/ Simon Hubardeau Jr. House
102 North Fourth St. at Jefferson St. (Private residence)

❖ Simon Hubardeau's family traveled from French Canada and settled in the original town of Ste. Genevieve. This c. 1789 Anglo-American limestone house, similar to the Eloy LeCompte House on North Main Street, was built by Jean Baptiste Hubardeau, Simon's son. It has no central hallway. The roof's original frame is intact. A fireplace mantel dating to the

COURTESY OF
VALERIE BATTLE KIENZLE

early 19th century is almost identical to a mantel in the Augustus Bequette House on Second Street. Additions and extensive exterior renovations have been made to the house and the vintage tin roof through the years. Of note are the *fleur-de-lis* (lily flower) cutouts on the house's shutters. In the Catholic church, the *fleur-de-lis* is associated with the Virgin Mary. Its three petals symbolize the Holy Trinity.

8 Hubardeau Icehouse
371 Jefferson St. (Rear of property, behind private residence)

❖ This c. 1817 Anglo-American limestone block structure was an outbuilding of the nearby Jean Baptiste Hubardeau House at North Fourth and Jefferson Streets. The ice pit inside the house has an earth floor. This relic of the days before commercial refrigeration was essential

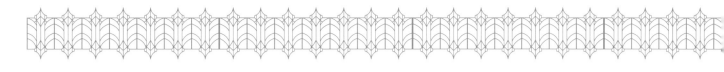

COURTESY OF VALERIE BATTLE KIENZLE

to the preservation of perishable food during Missouri's hot summer months. Large blocks of ice were harvested from the Mississippi River each winter and transported here by wagon. Layered with straw and stacked, these blocks could last for months while keeping food and beverage items cooled. The construction of this building is similar to that of the Thomure Icehouse.

9 Leon S. Yealy House
406 Jefferson St. (Private residence)

❖ This Italianate brick house was built in 1887. The foundation is made of limestone. Leon Yealy was a partner with Francis Jokerst and Charles Jokerst in the Jokerst-Yealy Mercantile Company, which was established in 1904. Their store was located at Merchant and Third Streets in 1906. It was rebuilt after burning in 1922, and was later leased by Rozier's Store.

COURTESY OF VALERIE BATTLE KIENZLE

10 Jacques Jean René Guibourd House/ Guibourd-Valle House
1 North Fourth St. and Merchant St.

❖ This house was constructed by former Frenchman Jacques Guibourd c. 1806 and features French Creole vertical log *poteaux-sur-sol* construction with *pierrotage*.

COURTESY OF VALERIE BATTLE KIENZLE

It has an open attic where visitors can see the house's Norman truss support system, featuring hand-hewn logs and wooden joining pins. The St. Louisans Jules Felix and Anne Marie Valle acquired the house in 1930 and restored it. Jules was a descendent of the Valle family. The house is a National Register property and today is owned by the Foundation for Restoration of Ste. Genevieve, a nonprofit organization established in 1967 for the purpose of promoting the preservation and restoration of Ste. Genevieve's historic structures. Some think the house is haunted.

11 Rear of Ste. Genevieve Catholic Church
49 Dubourg Pl. (Entrance is on South Fourth Street)

❖ Ste. Genevieve Parish is the oldest listed parish in what is now the Archdiocese of St. Louis and is the oldest in what is now the State of Missouri. It began keeping records in 1759. The main entrance to the church facilities is located around the corner on Dubourg Place and is part of Tour 3. The exterior of

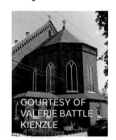

COURTESY OF VALERIE BATTLE KIENZLE

the hexagonal apse and two-sided transept altars date to 1911. It features intricate brickwork and artistic windows.

12 Judge Peter Huck House
15 South Fourth St. at Merchant St. (Private residence)

❖ This impressive Queen Anne–style stone house with ashlar walls and an octagonal tower was built c. 1908. It features stone columns and arched stone porch areas. It is part of the Ste. Genevieve Historic District. This home replaced the Charles Gregoire House on this lot. The original Gregoire house was a c. 1800 vertical log structure torn down in 1908. Charles Gregoire was born in France and is buried in Ste. Genevieve Memorial Cemetery. He was considered one of the area's leading citizens in 1820.

13 Gregoire House
71 South Fourth St.

❖ This painted brick Greek Revival house includes lots of interesting exterior and original interior architectural details. It dates to c. 1852–1861. The house's fireplaces are similar to those found in other nearby houses, including the Hertich House on North Main Street, the Joseph Govreau House on LeCompte, and the Valentine Rottler House on North Third Street.

 This concludes Tour 5. Continue on South Fourth Street. Turn right at South Fourth's intersection with Market Street. Follow Market for one block and turn right onto Fifth Street to return to your vehicle.

Bonus Driving Side Trips

Little Rock Landing ferry
COURTESY OF VALERIE BATTLE KIENZLE

Ste. Genevieve Levee Wildlife Refuge
Stormy Crawford Way

❖ The historic flood of 1993 brought devastation to Ste. Genevieve. From 1997 to 2001, an urban design levee was built by the US Army Corps of Engineers and floodwalls were installed to protect the historic city from future Mississippi River floodwaters. The Levee Trail is a packed gravel hiking trail along the

Levee floodgates
COURTESY OF VALERIE BATTLE KIENZLE

levee and the river. Land outside the levee is a wildlife refuge. What was true when famed 19th-century bird-watcher John James Audubon lived in Ste. Genevieve is true today: this area is a great place to observe birds and other wildlife. The refuge has a parking area near the end of Stormy Crawford Way, a short drive from downtown Ste. Genevieve. Essentials for a hike here include water, comfortable footwear, sun protection, first aid supplies, a navigational device (a compass or your cell phone's GPS), and a camera.

Little Rock Landing
8205 Little Rock Rd. at the Mississippi River

❖ Ste. Genevieve's first river ferry began crossing the Mississippi River about 1800, connecting it with Kaskaskia in what became Illinois (1818). Later, Little Rock Landing was the docking port for steamboats. *General Pike* was the first steamboat to arrive there in 1817. By 1904, railroad tracks were laid near the river and railroad cars were transported across the Mississippi by the ferry *Sainte Genevieve*. Tracks on

the ferry allowed it to accommodate rail cars. The ferry sank at Kellogg Landing in 1918. In 1922, a new rail car transfer operation was opened by the Missouri–Illinois Railroad. A new ferry, also called *Sainte Genevieve*, remained in operation until 1961. Today the Ste. Genevieve–Modoc Ferry (known locally as the French Connection) transports vehicles and passengers between Ste. Genevieve and Illinois sites such as Prairie du Rocher and Fort de Chartres. It operates year-round except during dangerous river conditions.

Pere Marquette City Park
North Main Street at Mathews Drive

❖ This picturesque park is located on the low hills near the levee and the Mississippi River. It opened in 1955 as the City Park and was renamed Pere Marquette Park in 1957. Marquette was the famous 17th-century French Jesuit missionary known as Father Jacques Marquette. The park features lots of open space, covered picnic areas, sports fields, a walking trail, and playground structures. It is dog-friendly and also has an 18-hole disc golf course.

COURTESY OF VALERIE BATTLE KIENZLE

Joseph Millard House
1007 North Main St. (Private residence)

❖ This large c. 1834 Federal double-pile house was built with dressed stone and roughly dressed fieldstone. It still contains what is thought to be much of its original vertical wooden supports and decorative wooden details. The house is located near the railroad tracks, the levee

COURTESY OF
LIBRARY OF CONGRESS,
PUBLIC DOMAIN

area, and Pere Marquette City Park. It was restored in the 1980s and saved from floodwater during 1993.

Pickle Springs Natural Area
22212 Dorlac Rd.

❖ The Missouri Department of Conservation oversees this National Natural Landmark. Pickle Springs Natural Area contains waterfalls, box canyons, rock formations, and unusual animals and plants. Hiking is available in the 250-plus-acre oasis, along with visual remnants from the time this area was covered with glaciers. A type of crustacean called an amphipod lives in Pickle Springs' waters. It is said to be unique to this area. Bird-watching also is a popular activity here. Pickle Springs Natural Area is located about 23 miles from downtown Ste. Genevieve.

Hawn State Park
12096 Park Rd.

❖ Located near Pickle Springs Natural Area and about 20 miles from downtown Ste. Genevieve, Hawn State Park's 4,956 acres feature a variety of hiking trails and camping and picnic facilities. Basic and electric campsites, as well as backpack and backcountry camping, are available. Acres of oak and pine trees, flowing streams, and sandstone cliffs and canyons make this natural wonder a favorite with Missouri outdoor enthusiasts. The park contains more than 600 species of trees, shrubs, wildflowers, and ferns. In addition, 156 bird species have been recorded in this park. An updated, downloadable bird checklist for Hawn State Park is available at *sparks.mobirds.org*.

Ste. Genevieve's Wine Country
(Route du Vin)

❖ Wine making has been an important part of the history of Missouri, and of Ste. Genevieve in particular, for generations. Early Ste. Geneviens made wine from wild grapes growing on vines in trees, as well as from local berries and fruits. Several vineyards, wineries, and a brewery are located within a short driving distance of downtown Ste. Genevieve. These include Cave Vineyard, Charleville Vineyards, Chaumette Brewery and Winery, and Crown Valley Winery. All are within close proximity to each other.

Tower Rock

❖ Tower Rock, also known as Grand Tower, is an island formation in the Mississippi River that is only fully visible during extreme drought conditions. It has been sited and noted by generations of visitors, including Native Americans, explorers Lewis and Clark, John James Audubon, and Mark Twain. Tower Rock is located in Perry County about 30 miles from Ste. Genevieve. In fall of 2022, record drought conditions diminished the river, revealing a somewhat walkable but treacherous rock path from the shore to the island. Observers flocked to the area for a chance to walk out to what is normally an island. A word of caution: due to the size and locations

COURTESY OF
THE STATE HISTORICAL
SOCIETY OF MISSOURI

of rocks that make up the path, not everyone should attempt the walk. The tower is located in a dangerous section of the river. The US Army Corps of Engineers wanted to eliminate the island in the 1870s. However, President Ulysses S. Grant remembered seeing Tower Rock and signed an executive order preserving it. It is listed in the National Register of Historic Places.

Afterword

The story of Ste. Genevieve is one with an overarching French theme but influenced by other peoples and cultures. Native Americans were friends, business partners, and sometimes enemies during the Colonial period. Enslaved Africans and their descendants toiled in the fields and mines throughout the Colonial period and the first 60 years of American rule.

Germans began immigrating en masse from 1832 to 1880 and left their mark on the food, religion, and architecture of the town. Steamboats and railroads facilitated the movements of goods to the rest of the nation and the world. Industrialization brought new ways to mine minerals and convert them into useful products. The arrival of electricity, telephones, and water and sewer systems brought the small city into the 20th century. The 2001 completion of the Urban Design Levee finally provided protection for the town and its historic buildings from the destruction of frequent Mississippi River floods.

While the town became Americanized during the last century, it never lost its enthusiasm for French traditions and customs. Celebrations of the city's founding and relocation, as well as annual festivals for *Le Bal*

Basil Misplait Well,
Old St. Marys Road
COURTESY OF
LIBRARY OF CONGRESS, PUBLIC DOMAIN

Du Roi/The King's Ball (held the first Saturday in February), *Jour de Fête* (held the second weekend in August), *La Guignolée* (held on New Year's Eve), the French Heritage Festival, and the Holiday Christmas Festival are highly anticipated.

But Ste. Genevieve was not always a collection of meticulously renovated historic buildings. By the mid-20th century, many of its buildings were in a state of disrepair and deterioration. Some early buildings had been razed. But thanks to the tireless efforts of concerned residents and preservationists, interest was generated in saving and revitalizing numerous historic structures. Ste. Genevieve did indeed have a fascinating 200-plus-year story to tell.

Today, Ste. Genevieve thrives. In 2020, three properties in the historic area became Ste. Genevieve National Historical Park, the 422nd unit of the National Park Service. In addition, parts have been included in a National Historic Landmark District designation and many properties are included in the National Register of Historic Places.

But Ste. Genevieve is not New Orleans; Colonial Williamsburg; St. Charles, Missouri; or any of the other well-preserved historic cities. It is a colorful French Creole river town that has survived, thrived, and continues to exist thanks to its residents and supporters. It has a rich history and a promising future!

COURTESY OF
VALERIE BATTLE KIENZLE

Acknowledgments

Thank you to **Bill Hart** for his dedication to the preservation of the fascinating history of Ste. Genevieve and the state of Missouri. He helps make history come alive for the rest of us.

Thank you to **Patrick Fehey, MD**, coproprietor with his wife **Susan O'Donnell, MD**, of Main Street Inn and the Antique Mall Ste. Genevieve. He is a hospitality host extraordinaire. The stories and wealth of Ste. Genevieve historical information he shares with guests are endearing this beautiful city to countless visitors.

Thank you to ASL Pewter owners, artisans, and historians **Tom and Pat Hooper** for sharing their artistic insights, vast historical knowledge, and a peek at their amazing 200-plus-year-old icehouse.

Thank you to **Robert Mueller**, independent researcher and local Ste. Genevieve historian, writer, and storyteller, for his assistance in reviewing this content for historical accuracy.

> **The present town of Ste. Genevieve is beautifully located on the verdant banks of the grand Mississippi, about sixty miles below the future great city of the world, St. Louis; and sits in beauty amid surrounding and smiling hills.**
>
> — FIRMAN A. ROZIER
>
> *Ste. Genevieve businessman and community leader at the 150th Anniversary Celebration of the Founding of Ste. Genevieve, July 21, 1885*

COURTESY OF
VALERIE BATTLE KIENZLE

COURTESY OF
VALERIE BATTLE KIENZLE

COURTESY OF LIBRARY
OF CONGRESS, PUBLIC DOMAIN

COURTESY OF
VALERIE BATTLE KIENZLE

TERMINUS

STE. GENEVIEVE
IRON MOUNTAIN & PILOT KNOB
PLANK ROAD

Sources

"150th Celebration of the Founding of Ste. Genevieve." Address by Firmin A. Rozier delivered to the City of Ste. Genevieve, MO, July 21, 1885.

"Archaeological Excavation at François Valle House, Ste. Genevieve, MO 10/1/16." Ste. Genevieve Community Access Television.

Basler, Lucille. *The District of Ste. Genevieve 1725–1980.* Ste. Genevieve, MO, 1980.

Brackenridge, Henry Marie. *Recollections of the Persons and Places in the West.* Philadelphia, PA: 1834.

Deposki, Richard. *Ste. Genevieve* (Images of America). Charleston, SC: Arcadia Publishing, 2008.

Ekberg, Carl J. *Colonial Ste. Genevieve: An Adventure on the Mississippi Frontier.* Gerald, MO: The Patrice Press, 1985.

Evans, Mark L. *The Commandant's Last Ride.* Cape Girardeau, MO: Ten-Digit Press, 2001.

Federal Writers' Project. *The WPA Guide to Missouri.* New York: Trinity University Press, 2013.

"Ferdinand Rozier (1777–1864)." *Missouri Encyclopedia, State Historical Society of Missouri.* https://missouriencyclopedia.org. Accessed July 28, 2023.

"François Valle." https://historicmissourians.shsmo.org/valle-francois. Accessed July 18, 2023.

Franzwa, Gregory M. *The Story of Old Ste. Genevieve—An Account of An Old French Town In Upper Louisiana: Its People and Their Homes,* Fifth Edition. St. Louis, MO: The Patrice Press, 1990.

"French-Canadian 'dit names' and nicknames." *Généalogie et Historie du Québec,* Institut Drouin, June 5, 2019.

"French Colonial America." Centre for French Colonial Life Museum; Ste. Genevieve, MO. www.frenchcolonialamerica.org, 2023.

_____. *Goodspeed's History of Southeast Missouri.* Chicago, IL: The Goodspeed Publishing Co., 1888.

Guitar, Sarah. "Monuments and Memorials in Missouri." *The Missouri Historical Review,* The State Historical Society of Missouri, July 1925.

"Hiking Trails in Ste. Genevieve, Missouri." Ste. Genevieve Welcome Center, Ste. Genevieve, MO, 2023.

"Historic Resources of Ste. Genevieve, Missouri." www.mostateparks.com/sites/mostateparks/files/HistoricResources-SteGenevieve.pdf.

"Kaskaskia & Mississippi Rivers, Confluence Heritage Area." Brochure. US Army Corps of Engineers, US Fish and Wildlife Service-Middle Mississippi River National Wildlife Refuge, Illinois Historic Preservation Agency-Randolph County Historic Sites, Randolph County-Chester Welcome Center, Ste. Genevieve Welcome Center, www.mvs.usace.army.mil/Portals/54/docs/recreation/kaskaskia/2013ConfluenceHeritage.pdf.

Kerr, Scott and Dick, R.H. *An American Art Colony: The Art and Artists of Ste. Genevieve, Missouri 1930–1940.* St. Louis, MO: McCaughen & Burr Press, 2004.

Library of Congress Prints and Photographs Division. "Historic American Buildings Survey (HABS)." Washington, DC. Accessed numerous times throughout 2023.

Library of Congress Prints and Photographs Division, "Prints by John James Audubon." Washington, DC. Accessed July 20, 2023.

Missouri Department of Natural Resources, Missouri State Parks, Hawn State Park brochure, 2023.

"Missouri Winery Guide." Missouri Wine and Grape Board, 2022.

Morrow, Lynn. *A Surveyor's Challenges: P.K. Robbins in Missouri.* Cape Girardeau, MO: Southeast Missouri State University Press, 2006.

Naeger, Bill and Patti and Evans, Mark L. *Ste. Genevieve–A Leisurely Stroll through History.* Ste. Genevieve, MO: Merchant St. Publishing, 1999.

National Park Service, US Department of the Interior, "Ste. Genevieve Final Special Resource Study and Environmental Assessment, Missouri." May 2016. https://parkplanning.nps.gov/document

Overby, Ozment. Foreword, *The Commandant's Last Ride.* Cape Girardeau, MO: Ten-Digit Press, 2001.

Rozier, Firmin A. *Rozier's History of the Early Settlement of the Mississippi Valley.* St Louis, MO: G.A. Pierrot & Sons, 1890.

"Sainte Geneviève." The Historical Marker Database, State Historical Society of Missouri and State Highway Commission, 1953. www.hmdb.org

Schaaf, Ida M. "The Founding of Ste. Genevieve, Missouri." *Missouri Historical Review,* Vol. 27, Issue 2, January 1933.

Schroeder, Walter A. *Opening the Ozarks.* Columbia, MO: University of Missouri Press, 2002.

"Ste. Genevieve Architectural Survey." Missouri State Parks. https://mostateparks.com/sites/mostateparks/files/Ste.%20Genevieve%20Survey.pdf

"Ste. Genevieve County Courthouse." www.extension.missouri.edu. Accessed March 30, 2023.

Ste. Genevieve Fair Play, June 14, 1872; July 16, 1880; Jan. 21, 1888; 1888; May 17, 1890; and other issues.

Ste. Genevieve Herald. Dec. 2, 2020; May 4, 2022; and other issues.

"Ste. Genevieve Historic District." https://mostateparks.com/sites/mostateparks/files/Ste-Genevieve_HD.pdf. 2012

"Ste. Genevieve, Missouri." www.visitstegen.com. Accessed January 2023.

"Ste. Genevieve National Historical Park." www.nps.gov.

"Ste. Genevieve National Historical Park." www.parkrangerjohn.com

Stepenoff, Bonnie. "Faire une Maison: Carpenters in Ste. Genevieve, 1750–1850." *The Confluence,* Lindenwood University, Spring/Summer 2014.

Stevens, Walter B., *Centennial History of Missouri,* Vol. 2, St. Louis, MO: The S.J. Clarke Publishing Co., 1921.

Thomas, Sue. *A Second Home: Missouri's Early Schools.* Columbia, MO: University of Missouri Press, 2006.

"Treasure of Land and Lore." *Our Mississippi,* US Army Corps of Engineers, Spring 2023.

US Department of the Interior, National Park Service, National Register of Historic Places, "Ste. Genevieve Green Tree Tavern" brochure.

Wehmeyer, Janice C. *Ste. Genevieve, MO: A Guided Tour through the Past and Present.* Ste. Genevieve, MO: Fair Play Printing Co., 1993.

Weiser, Kathy. "Legends of America," Nov. 2020. Retrieved Feb. 8, 2023. www.legendsofamerica.com/mo-steGenevieve/

"Welcome to Sainte Geneviève Parish," The Historical Marker Database. Retrieved March 22, 2023. www.hmdb.org

"Where the Curious Learn." Sainte Genevieve Museum Learning Center brochure, 2023.

Yealy, Francis J., S.J. *Sainte Genevieve: The Story of Missouri's Oldest Settlement.* Ste. Genevieve, MO: Ste. Genevieve Bicentennial Historical Commission, 1935.

Index